G000095469

Business archival sources for the local historian

Maynooth Research Guides for Irish Local History

GENERAL EDITOR Mary Ann Lyons

This book is one of the Maynooth Research Guides for Irish Local History series. Written by specialists in the relevant fields, these volumes are designed to provide historians, and especially those interested in local history, with practical advice regarding the consultation of specific collections of historical materials, thereby enabling them to conduct independent research in a competent and thorough manner. In each volume, a brief history of the relevant institutions is provided and the principal primary sources are identified and critically evaluated with specific reference to their usefulness to the local historian. Readers receive step by step guidance as to how to conduct their research and are alerted to some of the problems which they might encounter in working with particular collections. Possible avenues for research are suggested and relevant secondary works are also recommended.

The General Editor acknowledges the assistance of both Professor Raymond Gillespie, NUI Maynooth and Professor James Kelly, St Patrick's College, Drumcondra, in the preparation of this book for publication.

IN THIS SERIES

1 Terence A.M. Dooley, *Sources for the history of landed estates in Ireland* (2000)
2 Raymond Refaussé, *Church of Ireland records* (2nd ed., 2006)
3 Patrick J. Corish and David C. Sheehy, *Records of the Irish Catholic Church* (2001)
4 Philomena Connolly, *Medieval record sources* (2002)
5 Brian Gurrin, *Pre-census sources for Irish demography* (2002)
6 E. Margaret Crawford, *Counting the people: a survey of the Irish censuses, 1813–1911* (2003)
7 Brian Hanley, *A guide to the Irish military heritage* (2004)
8 Jacinta Prunty, *Maps and map-making in local history* (2004)
9 Brian Griffin, *Sources for the study of crime in Ireland, 1801–1921* (2005)
10 Toby Barnard, *A guide to sources for the history of material culture in Ireland, 1500–2000* (2005)
11 Terence Dooley, *The big houses and landed estates of Ireland: a research guide* (expanded and updated edition of no. 1 in this series; 2007)
12 Patrick J. Duffy, *Exploring the history and heritage of Irish landscapes* (2007)
13 Liam Kelly, *Photographs and photography in Irish local history* (2008)
14 Katharine Simms, *Medieval Gaelic sources* (2009)
15 C.J. Woods, *Travellers' accounts as source-material for Irish historians* (2009)
16 Ciarán Ó hÓgartaigh and Margaret Ó hÓgartaigh, *Business archival sources for the local historian* (2010)

Maynooth Research Guides for Irish Local History: Number 16

Business archival sources for the local historian

15/4/2010

Ciarán Ó hÓgartaigh and Margaret Ó hÓgartaigh

Margaret Ó hÓgartaigh, (To Andrea Ward) my great neighbour, Margaret.

Mr Whitiam (a shed)

FOUR COURTS PRESS

Set in 10.5 pt on 12.5 pt Bembo for
FOUR COURTS PRESS LTD
7 Malpas Street, Dublin 8
www.fourcourtspress.ie
and in North America by
FOUR COURTS PRESS
c/o ISBS, 920 N.E. 58th Avenue, Suite 300, Portland, OR 97213

© Ciarán Ó hÓgartaigh and Margaret Ó hÓgartaigh & Four Courts Press 2010

A catalogue record for this title
is available from the British Library.

ISBN 978–1–84682–133–2 hbk
978–1–84682–134–9 pbk

All rights reserved. No part of this publication may be
reproduced, stored in or introduced into a retrieval system,
or transmitted, in any form or by any means (electronic,
mechanical, photocopying, recording or otherwise),
without the prior written permission of the
copyright owner.

Printed in England
by MPG Books Ltd, Bodmin, Cornwall.

Contents

Illustrations

Acknowledgments

Our thanks to all those who helped us during the course of writing this book, Ciara Breathnach, Brain Donnelly, Brendan Twomey, Neal Garnham, Finola Kennedy, Liam Kennedy, Margaret MacCurtain and Joanna Wydenbach. Amir Abdullah Awan provided invaluable assistance in sourcing references in University College Dublin library. We are particularly indebted to Louis Cullen who was inspirational.

The staff at the National Library, the National Archives, the Public Record Office of Northern Ireland and the Gilbert Library went out of their way to help us, particularly Máire Kennedy at the Gilbert Library and Bernard Devaney, Sandra McDermott and Colette O'Daly at the National Library of Ireland.

We are grateful for the continued generosity of Irish Accountancy Educational Trust. It supported the construction of our database which forms the basis of this book. The cover photograph is courtesy of J.J. O'Beirne of Blackrock Market. Mary Ann Lyons was an exemplary editor and we are grateful to everyone at Four Courts Press.

For our parents
and Professor Louis Cullen

CHAPTER I

Business archives and the historian

This chapter begins by highlighting the importance of evidence and the archive in historical research. The engagement of Irish historians with the accounting and business fields and the work to date in business history in Ireland is then explored. In order to convey the richness of archival collections relating to various categories of businesses and to provide an overview of the major classifications of such material in the National Archives of Ireland and in the Public Record Office of Northern Ireland, section three describes the database of accounting and corporate governance archives[1] compiled as part of this research project and discusses its potential contribution to historical research. Thereafter a methodological context is set out for historians' consultation and analysis of business archives, highlighting the unique value of unexplored archival material in deepening our understanding of the past.

BUSINESS ARCHIVES

Archives represent a collection of public, personal or corporate documents or records. They may comprise the personal papers of an individual, or the records of a public body such as a Department of State or a local authority, or the records of another institution such as a business, society, club, union or religious organization. Archival collections take many forms, including correspondence, diaries, files, minutes of meetings, reports, legal documents, bills or invoices, photographs, maps, plans and drawings, account books, audio, visual, and electronic records. The major repositories of business and other archives in Ireland are the National Archives of Ireland (NAI) in Dublin and the Public Record Office of Northern Ireland (PRONI) in Belfast. Until the opening of the NAI in January 1991, there were

1 The archives outlined in this book are described as relating to both accounting and corporate governance as many of the records include non-accounting material such as minute books, correspondence, details of shareholders and other such records. We argue that these records may be useful in shedding light on issues pertaining to corporate governance and organizational change. Furthermore, the National Archives of Ireland [hereinafter NAI] and the Public Record of Northern Ireland [hereinafter PRONI] – and indeed other archives identified here – also contain significant material relating to taxation and, in the Dissolved Companies files, records relating to corporate failure and liquidation. These are not addressed in detail in this book as they are outside the scope of the database featured in Appendix 1.

two main archives in the Republic of Ireland: the Public Record Office at the Four Courts in Dublin and the State Paper Office at Dublin Castle. Despite heroic efforts by some of the archivists, these repositories were inadequate and grossly underfunded. Conversely, the Public Record Office of Northern Ireland (PRONI) soon became a byword for administrative efficiency and an enlightened collections policy, particularly under its first director, D.A. Chart, himself a distinguished historian as well as an enthusiastic archivist.[2]

Since 1970 records acquired by the Business Records Survey of the Irish Manuscripts Commission have been deposited in the NAI. In the early 1970s, following a pilot survey of business records in Dundalk and Drogheda conducted by Brian Trainor of the PRONI and Marie Smith of the UCD Library School, 'the most systematic and thorough' survey of records in the Republic of Ireland was carried out. It fortuitously coincided with the early stages of an economic boom in Ireland: 'consequently the survey's launch coincided with or preceded re-organization in many firms or a move to new premises'. The survey was originally administered by the Business Records Committee of the Irish Manuscripts Commission under the chairmanship of R.D. Edwards, together with two joint directors, Breandán MacGiolla Choille and L.M. Cullen. (The current surveyor is Brian Donnelly of the NAI.)[3] Also fortuitous was the fact that from its inception in the mid-1970s the Economic and Social History Society of Ireland sought to preserve business papers.[4]

In 1983 L.M. Cullen reported on the wide variety of businesses approached during the course of the survey, ranging from solicitors' offices to hospitals. Down to 1982 a total of 5,239 firms had been approached in order to ascertain whether they had non-current business records. 'Of these, 1,105 or 21 per cent [had] non-current records; and, of these, 435 [had] made deposits' to the archives. Hence, while the survey of business records was comprehensive in scale, the availability of the actual records in repositories depends on the survival and condition of such records and on the willingness of the firm to deposit the material in archives. Cullen has also alerted historians to the wide-ranging and occasionally surprising research possibilities that business records can offer. He suggests that, in 'addition to their relevance for the study of localities or businesses [business records] may prove useful for the study of less explicit issues, ranging from accounting and literacy, to the types of stationery and ledgers in use, and to the frequency of retail or credit transactions.' Indeed, Cullen's suggestion provided the stimulus for the present authors' recent study of accounting and literacy in eighteenth-century Ireland.[5]

2 Seán Magee, 'D.A. Chart, 1878–1960: archivist, historian, social scientist' in *History Ireland* (Spring 2003), pp 15–18.   **3** L.M. Cullen, 'Irish Manuscripts Commission survey of business records' in *Irish Economic & Social History*, 10 (1983), pp 81–5: pp 82–3.   **4** L.M. Cullen, 'Hon. Secretary's report' in *Irish Economic & Social History*, 1 (1974), pp 71–4: p. 71.   **5** Cullen, 'Irish Manuscripts Commission survey of business records', pp 84–5; Ciarán Ó hÓgartaigh and Margaret Ó hÓgartaigh, 'Teaching accounting in eighteenth-century Ireland' in Felix Larkin (ed.), *Librarians, poets and scholars: a festschrift for Dónall Ó Luanaigh*

In the 1980s steps were taken to enhance the archival stores in the Irish Republic. The need to find room for the vast quantity of archival material produced by various government departments was recognized in 1986 when, with the support of the Taoiseach of the time, Garret FitzGerald (himself an economic historian), the National Archives Act was passed. The Act requires that all official documents produced by the State had to be deposited at the National Archives which is now regarded as the main repository for official documents in Ireland. Researchers should, however, be mindful that business archives that are of interest to the local historian may also be found in other national and local archives, as well as in local or private custody and these are discussed in more detail at relevant points throughout this guide.

HISTORIANS AND BUSINESS AND ACCOUNTING RECORDS

Historians have engaged with accounting and business archives primarily in the areas of social and economic history. While much economic and social history draws on macro-economic data, micro-level and firm-level sources have cast new light on historical crises such as the Great Famine and broad themes including the development of trade both within Ireland and between Ireland and other countries. Cormac Ó Gráda, for example, utilized estate records – and the levels of debt evidenced therein – to suggest that landlords did not invariably emerge as beneficiaries from the Great Famine of 1845–9.[6] In his study of the brandy trade during the *ancien regime* era, L.M. Cullen draws upon business archives held in the National Library of Ireland and the National Archives of Ireland. Furthermore, in his work on eighteenth-century Ireland Cullen alludes to Irish 'counting houses' in Continental Europe. A counting house, or compting house, was the building or room(s) in which merchants (and later businesses more generally) carried on their accounting operations. Such locales may be of particular interest to local historians since Cullen presents evidence that members of specific families, such as the Bellews of Mountbellew, County Galway, attended these 'counting houses' of Europe.[7]

Since the 1980s a substantial corpus of corporate histories has also developed, including Tony Farmar's histories of Bewley's, Holles Street hospital, and Heiton's,[8] L.M. Cullen's history of Eason's,[9] S.R. Dennison and Oliver

(Dublin, 2007), pp 185–94. **6** Cormac Ó Gráda, *Black '47 and beyond: the Great Irish Famine in history, economy and memory* (Princeton, 1999). **7** L.M. Cullen, *The brandy trade under the ancien regime* (Cambridge, 1998) and idem, 'Catholic social classes under the Penal Laws' in T.P. Power and Kevin Whelan (eds), *Endurance and emergence: Catholics in Ireland in the eighteenth century* (Dublin, 1990), pp 57–84. **8** Tony Farmar, *A history of Craig Gardner: the first 100 years* (Dublin, 1988); idem, *Holles Street 1894–1994: the National Maternity Hospital – a centenary history* (Dublin, 1994); idem, *Heitons – a managed transition* (Dublin, 1996). **9** L.M. Cullen, *Eason & Son: a history* (Dublin, 1989).

McDonagh's history of Guinness[10] and the history of Jacob's, the biscuit manufacturers, published by Séamus Ó Maitiú.[11] Each of these corporate institutions had
particular social and economic significance for the local community in which they
operated, often serving as an interface between the local, the national and, at times,
the international. Furthermore, several institutional histories, published since the
late 1990s, have relied to varying extents on accounting and corporate governance
records. For example, Diarmaid Ferriter's work on local authorities in Limerick and
Mary E. Daly's histories of government departments draw, *inter alia*, on government records to illuminate and elucidate their understanding of the role of government at local and national levels, together with its institutions, in twentieth-
century Ireland.[12]

The collections held by the NAI inevitably serve as both inspiration and impetus to such scholarly studies. However, interestingly in the context of contemporary commentary and debate in Irish society, histories of more controversial
institutions such as orphanages and industrial schools – while making claims regarding the financial wealth but moral ill-health of those institutions[13] – have tended
not to draw significantly on accounting and business archives. This may be attrib-
uted to the power of oral history concerning life in such institutions and also to
increasingly restricted access to their archives in recent years.

While histories of business institutions have, therefore, been relatively plentiful,
studies by historians of the business professions have been less numerous and have
been undertaken more as a means to understand the context – both local and
national – in which professionals operated and less as studies of the professions in
their own right. Dáire Hogan's histories of the legal profession in Ireland are cases
in point.[14]

Margaret Ó hÓgartaigh's work on the engineering, pharmaceutical, medical
and dental professions as well as Ciarán Ó hÓgartaigh and Margaret Ó
hÓgartaigh's brief history of early female accountants focus in particular on the role
of women in these professions and the manner in which professional structures
established a boundary within which women operated.[15]

10 S.R. Dennison and Oliver McDonagh, *Guinness, 1886–1939: from incorporation to the
Second World War* (Cork, 1998).   11 Séamus Ó Maitiú, *W. & R. Jacob: celebrating 150 years
of Irish biscuit making* (Dublin, 2001).   12 Diarmaid Ferriter, *Cuimhnigh ar Luimneach: a history of Limerick County Council, 1898–1998* (Limerick, 1998); M.E. Daly, *The buffer State: the
historical roots of the Department of the Environment* (Dublin, 1997) and eadem, *The first
Department: a history of the Department of Agriculture* (Dublin, 2002).   13 Eoin O'Sullivan and
Mary Raftery, *Suffer the little children: the inside story of Ireland's industrial schools* (Dublin,
1999).   14 Dáire Hogan, *The legal profession in Ireland, 1789–1922* (Dublin, 1986); idem (ed.),
Brehons, serjeants and attorneys: studies in the history of the Irish legal profession (Dublin, 1990).
15 Margaret Ó hÓgartaigh, '"Am I a lady or an engineer?" Early Irish female engineers' in
The Engineers' Journal (Dec. 2002), pp 48–9; eadem, 'Women in pharmacy in the early twentieth century' in *The Irish Pharmacy Journal*, 82:6 (June 2004), pp 273–8; eadem, '"Is there
any need of you?" Women in medicine in Ireland and Australia' in *Australian Journal of Irish
Studies*, 4 (2004), pp 162–71; eadem, 'Women in Irish dentistry' in *Journal of the Irish Dental*

Accounting historians and historians

General history[16] and accounting history can be differentiated on the basis of their focus. Accounting history is concerned with the nature and implications of accounting change while history's focus is necessarily wider, centering on a broader social, political and economic canvass: in the latter case, accounting and corporate governance archives are of specific interest, casting unique light on that broader canvass. Whereas the professional histories of Ó hÓgartaigh and Cullen focus on the impact of the professions and of professionalization on the wider social context (such as on women), histories of the accounting profession *per se* have explored the impact of the wider context on the profession: the profession itself has been the *dramatis persona*. This is evident in the case of Henry Robinson's well-known and somewhat acritical *History of accountants in Ireland*[17] and in David Rowe's collection of edited essays to commemorate the centenary of the foundation of the Institute of Chartered Accountants in Ireland (ICAI).[18] Marcia Annisette and Philip O'Regan provide a more critical, contextual analysis of the early years of the ICAI, exploring the political and religious milieu of the period.[19] This broader canvass is also reflected in Peter Clarke's description of the development of financial reporting in Ireland which goes beyond study of the profession itself to observe the 'economic, social and political factors' which influenced the development of accounting in Ireland in a 'period of independent isolation'.[20] Clarke's paper, which offers a 'glimpse' at some early Irish accounting texts, is worth noting.[21] Alongside histories of the macro-professional level there have been micro-histories of accounting firms such as Farmar's aforementioned *History of Craig Gardner*. This company setting is also addressed by E.A. French in his work on the origins of general limited liability in the United Kingdom, which features reference to limited liability companies in Ireland.[22]

In his study of accountability and financial control as 'patriotic' strategies in late seventeenth and early eighteenth-century Ireland, Philip O'Regan uses business

Association, 51:4 (Winter 2005), pp 185–6; eadem and Ciarán Ó hÓgartaigh, 'A man's trousers on' in *Accountancy Ireland* (Sept. 1999), pp 22–3.   **16** The term 'history' is ambiguous in English and many other languages, meaning – on the one hand – *res gestae* or the course of human events and – on the other – *historia rerum gestarum* or the reports of those human events rendered by historians. Throughout this guide, the term 'history' is used in the latter sense.   **17** Henry Robinson, *A history of accountants in Ireland* (Dublin, 1964); idem, *A history of accountants in Ireland* (2nd ed., Dublin, 1983).   **18** David Rowe (ed.), *The Irish chartered accountant: centenary essays, 1888–1988* (Dublin, 1988).   **19** Marcia Annisette and Philip O'Regan, 'The survival of an All Ireland institution: the case of the Institute of Chartered Accountants of Ireland', paper presented at the Critical Perspectives in Accounting Conference, Apr. 2002, New York, available at http://aux.zicklin.baruch.cuny.edu/critical/   **20** Peter Clarke, 'Financial reporting in Ireland: the period of independent isolation' in *The Irish Accounting Review*, 8:2 (2001), pp 23–44: p. 23.   **21** Peter Clarke, 'A glimpse at Irish accounting history' in *Irish Accounting Review*, 3:2 (1996), pp 23–40.   **22** E.A. French, 'The origin of general limited liability in the United Kingdom' in *Accounting & Business Research*, 21:81 (1990), pp 15–34.

and accounting archives to construct a thematic interpretation of political events in that era, and in the process, successfully marries political and accounting history.[23] Ingrid Jeacle and Eamonn Walsh's accomplished exploration of the implications of introducing accounting and control systems in a Dublin department store is a particularly valuable study in contextualization of accounting during an age of consumption.[24] These scholarly contributions represent important recent developments in defining Irish accounting historiography. They reflect attempts by the community of accounting historians to place the structure and professionalization of accounting in a wider socio-economic interpretative framework, recognizing that professions organize principally to advance and defend members' interests and that they are also not impervious to the influences and pressures of the socio-political environment of which they are part.[25] These advances also represent early if somewhat sporadic shoots of a 'new accounting history' in Ireland which, according to Ó hÓgartaigh, Ó hÓgartaigh and Jeacle, aims

> to gain deeper insights into new practices, accounting researchers responded by tailoring their methodological approach and surveying their fields of inquiry from broader perspectives. The importance of historical context increasingly emerged as a key issue of late twentieth-century accounting research. Whilst historical accounting research is not a new phenomenon, it became infused in recent decades with a wider conception of the social world in which accounting operates.[26]

Indeed, as will be shown in chapter 3, accounting records can provide a wealth of information for the historian interested in re-constructing an image of the economic and social life of a local community.

The equivalent defining moment for 'new accounting history' occurred in 1991 with the publication of an edition of the journal *Accounting, Organizations and Society* devoted to the topic. The introductory article by Peter Miller, Trevor Hopper and Richard Laughlin argues that the more prominent role which accounting history has played within the accounting discipline during recent years, and the different focus and scope of this work to that which has been traditionally used in accounting history, has given accounting historians a justification for refer-

---

23 Philip O'Regan, 'Accountability and financial control as "Patriotic" strategies: accomptants and the Public Accounts Committee in late seventeenth and early eighteenth-century Ireland' in *Accounting Historians Journal*, 30:2 (2003), pp 105–32.   **24** Ingrid Jeacle and Eamon Walsh, 'From moral evaluation to rationalization: accounting and the shifting technologies of credit' in *Accounting, Organizations and Society*, 27 (2002), pp 737–61.   **25** Stephen J. Walker and Ken Shackleton, 'A ring fence for the profession. Advancing the closure of British accountancy, 1957–1970' in *Accounting, Auditing and Accountability Journal*, 11:1 (1998), pp 34–71; Stephen J. Walker, 'Accounting in history' in *Accounting Historians Journal*, 33:2 (2005), pp 233–59.   **26** Ciarán Ó hÓgartaigh, Margaret Ó hÓgartaigh and Ingrid Jeacle, '"How it essentially was": truth claims in history and accounting' in *Accounting Historians Journal*, 29:1 (2001), pp 42–67.

ring to 'the new accounting history'.[27] They highlight some of the characteristics of this new approach. It is interdisciplinary in nature, covering numerous disciplines including social, political, legal and economic. Classic examples of such studies are the work of Stuart Burchell, Colin Clubb and Anthony Hopwood on the growing interest in value-added accounting in the United Kingdom during the 1970s, Anne Loft's examination of the emergence of the cost accounting profession in the UK during the period from 1914 to 1925, Peter Miller and Ted O'Leary's study of standard costing and budgeting during the early years of the twentieth century and Anthony Hopwood's exploration of three case studies of accounting change.[28]

THE BUSINESS ARCHIVE AS HISTORICAL SOURCE FOR THE LOCAL HISTORIAN

A business archive should be interrogated with reference to the context in which it was created and preserved. In addition, the historian has to be mindful that as with all historical sources, business documents were generated for a specific reason or reasons and that they offer a perspective on historical events and personalities. The construction of business records and accounts is traditionally characterized in business and economics as posing what are termed 'agency (or principal-agent) problems'. The agent manages the business or the business function on behalf of somebody else ('the principal'), for example, the shareholder. The principal monitors the agent through inspection of financial statements, accounts or other written reports. In reporting to the principal, the agent may, therefore, have very specific motivations in presenting his/her account, perspective or point of view. Although this account survives in the archive, the context and the motivation are lost. It is also important to be mindful that just as history is usually written by winners, business sources are often generated by the moneyed classes (the 'economic winners') and, as a consequence, necessarily record a particular point of view. Therefore, in examining business sources, there are several issues which researchers are well advised to address. Generation of the historical, accounting source 'creates a reality': the author includes and omits information, presents it in a certain way, and thereby 'creates a picture of an organization'.[29] Accounting numbers have an

27 Peter Miller, Trevor Hopper and Richard Laughlin, 'The new accounting history: an introduction' in *Accounting, Organizations and Society*, 16:3 (1991), pp 395–403: p. 395. **28** Stuart Burchell, Colin Clubb and Anthony G. Hopwood, 'Accounting in its social context: towards a history of value-added in the United Kingdom' in *Accounting, Organizations and Society*, 10 (1985), pp 381–413; Anne Loft, 'Towards a critical understanding of accounting: the case of cost accounting in the U.K., 1914–1925' in *Accounting, Organizations and Society*, 11 (1986), pp 137–71; Peter Miller and Timothy O'Leary, 'Accounting and the construction of the governable person' in *Accounting, Organizations and Society*, 12 (1987), pp 235–66; Anthony G. Hopwood, 'The archaeology of accounting systems' in *Accounting, Organizations and Society*, 12 (1987), pp 207–34. **29** Ruth D. Hines, 'Financial accounting: in communicating reality, we construct reality' in *Accounting, Organizations and Society*, 13 (1988), pp 251–61.

aura of certainty but readers – historians in particular – should not assume that they are 'objective'. The source ought to be interrogated with an eye to the possible or probable perspective of its creator, the intended audience, the purpose and the context in which it was written. Historians of accounting archives also need to monitor the extent to which material in the collection has been changed or reorganized over time. Furthermore, given that business records tend on the whole to be voluntarily deposited in archives, researchers need to be alert to limitations arising from the inevitably selective nature of those accessions.

Accounting sources may be written as a form of account by a sole trader (accounting to him or herself), a clerk (to a superior), an agent (to an owner), a manager (to a shareholder), an organization (for public or official consumption) or an individual (for posterity).[30] Business sources – including financial statements – are not necessarily faithful representations of the past but they are none the less a representation of the state of affairs at a specific time and for a specific purpose. These factors are characterized as 'agency problems' in accounting, the agent being motivated to report to the principal in a certain way, depending on the principal-agent relationship.[31] For example, the financial statements of a company may report a level of profit for tax purposes. An agent may wish to portray a particular outcome for the landlord. Credit rating comments addressed by a clerk to his or her manager may offer a justification for entering (or indeed not entering) into a specific transaction. On the other hand, a newsagent may simply wish to record particular transactions with a view to maintaining adequate stock levels. For the local historian with a special interest in small businesses, accounting information used for internal decision-making purposes – conventionally termed management accounting – is likely to be the most informative source as accounting to oneself does not pose principal-agent problems in the conventional sense.

An historian working with an historical business source ought to be guided by auditing standards which advise that 'the reliability of audit evidence is influenced by its source and by its nature and is dependent on the individual circumstances under which it is obtained'.[32] Furthermore, in general, the auditor privileges external sources of information over those produced by or within the organization. Reflecting this approach, the Auditing Standard on audit evidence states:

> While recognizing that exceptions may exist, the following generalizations about the reliability of audit evidence may be useful:

30 Accounting information used for internal financial decisions (by management) is termed 'management accounting'. Accounting information which assists those external those to the company in making decisions is generally termed 'financial accounting'.   **31** Sheila Marriner, 'Company financial statements as source material for business historians' in *Business History*, 22 (1980), pp 203–35; Tom Lee, 'The changing form of the Corporate Annual Report' in *Accounting Historians Journal*, 21:1 (1994), pp 215–34; Patti Mills, 'Agency, auditing and the unregulated environment: some further historical evidence' in *Accounting, Auditing and Accountability Journal*, 3:1 (1990), pp 54–66.   **32** Auditing Practices Board, International Standard on Auditing (UK & Ireland) 500 *Audit Evidence*, para. 9.

- Audit evidence is more reliable when it is obtained from independent sources outside the entity;
- Audit evidence that is generated internally is more reliable when the related controls imposed by the entity are effective;
- Audit evidence obtained directly by the auditor (for example, observation of the application of a control) is more reliable than audit evidence obtained indirectly or by inference (for example, inquiry about the application of a control);
- Audit evidence is more reliable when it exists in documentary form, whether paper, electronic, or other medium (for example, a contemporaneously written record of a meeting is more reliable than a subsequent oral representation of the matters discussed);
- Audit evidence provided by original documents is more reliable than audit evidence provided by photocopies or facsimiles.[33]

On the basis of this advice, archival evidence drawn from sources that are external to the business, such as bills, invoices, statements of account and letters, are in general to be relied upon to a greater extent than sources generated by personnel within the business itself. Indeed, these external records can be especially informative in their own right, with architects' and contractors' bills often yielding valuable evidence on the original site for a particular building, details of its renovation and the cost of construction. Furthermore, the internal records of a business – the original accounting entries in ledger accounts – which were written for internal consumption are potentially more reliable than financial or other statements produced for a specific purpose (taxation or other reasons). Adjustments to accounts or notes in the margins of accounting records are worthy of attention. These represent additions or amendments to the routine which can provide insights into particular motivations or 'stories' which will not be revealed in unvarnished accounting records alone.

In summary, like all archival material accounting records are not an unbiased source and researchers need to be mindful of the agendas that shaped the creation of these records as Sheila Marriner has emphasized in her review of the use of company financial statements as source material for business historians:[34]

> The evaluation of such records by anyone without accounting training *is* fraught with dangers. The battery of criticisms that can be directed against their accuracy, reliability and consistency is so intense that one might be tempted to conclude that they contain no useful information at all. If, however, a complete range of a business's accounting records is not available it is tempting to try and squeeze something out of published financial state-

33 Auditing Practices Board, International Standard on Auditing (UK & Ireland) 500 *Audit Evidence*, para. 9. **34** Marriner, 'Company financial statements as source material for business historians', in *Business History*, 22 (1980), pp 203–35.

ments, and they *can* contribute to an understanding of a business's history if the historian has a thorough understanding of their *raison d'être*, of the extent to which their meaning and content have varied (as statutory requirements changed and as a body of case law was built up to interpret statutory requirements), and if the historian fully acknowledges their many serious defects.

CHAPTER 2

Archives and sources

This chapter briefly outlines the history of systematic organization and surveying of business records in the National Archives of Ireland (NAI),[1] the Public Record Office of Northern Ireland (PRONI)[2] and other repositories since the early 1970s. Readers are provided with an introduction to the electronic database of business archives in the NAI and PRONI compiled by the authors of this guide.[3] Particularly relevant reports, guides and information sheets produced by these institutions are evaluated in terms of their usefulness to local historians. The main categories of business records (or archives holding business material) are also identified.

BUSINESS ARCHIVES CATALOGUED

As mentioned in chapter 1, the first – and seminal – survey of business records in the Republic of Ireland was undertaken by the Irish Manuscripts Commission and led by L.M. Cullen, commencing on 1 September 1970. Cullen comments that this was an 'auspicious' period to embark on the cataloguing task as 'the economic boom in the Republic was in its early stages: consequently the survey's launching coincided with or preceded re-organization of many firms or a move to new premises'.[4] Many of the archives featured in the survey were deposited in what is now the National Archives of Ireland or in the Public Record Office of Northern Ireland during the 1970s and 1980s and there have been regular accessions since. The 'outstanding individual deposits' were those of Irish Distillers Limited dating back to 1777, which are now in the collections of the NAI and Cork Archives Council.[5] In 1983 Cullen con-

1 The National Archives of Ireland, Bishop Street, Dublin 8, Republic of Ireland. Tel.: +353 (0)1 407 2300/LoCall:+ 353 1890 252424, Fax:+353 (0)1 407 2333, E-mail: mail@nationalarchives.ie. For details of opening hours, access and frequently asked questions, see http://www.nationalarchives.ie/index.html. 2 Public Record Office of Northern Ireland, 66 Balmoral Avenue, Belfast BT9 6NY, Northern Ireland. Tel.: +44 (0)28 9025 5905, Fax: +44 (0)28 9025 5999, E-mail: proni@dcalni.gov.uk. For details of opening hours, access and frequently asked questions, see http://www.proni.gov.uk/index.htm. 3 Ciarán Ó hÓgartaigh and Margaret Ó hÓgartaigh, 'Business archives in the National Archives of Ireland and the Public Record Office of Northern Ireland: a *mappa mundi*' in *Irish Economic & Social History*, 31 (2004), pp 61–8. 4 Cullen, 'The Irish Manuscripts Commission survey of business records', pp 81–2. Our thanks to Louis Cullen for pointing out that these records also tell us a lot about business conditions during the period of cataloguing, in particular, the economic problems faced by businesses in the 1970s and 1980s. 5 Cork City Archives: Archivist: Brian McGee, Seamus Murphy Building,

cluded that 'some collections are sufficient to provide the backbone of major studies of an industry or even a firm.'[6] Milling is the best represented industry sector, with some local mills featuring prominently: R. & H. Hall has records for local mills in Dublin, Cork and Waterford (the latter since 1777).[7] Similarly, Guinness holds a range of provincial collections, some which are in the NAI.[8]

Building on the early work of the survey of business records and drawing on the annual reports compiled by Brian Donnelly (business archivist at the National Archives) and others, a research project was undertaken by the authors of this guide in 2002, funded by the Irish Accountancy Educational Trust (IAET).[9] It set out to establish and disseminate through the use of new technologies a database of accounting and corporate governance archives in the NAI and the PRONI.[10] The database, completed in 2004, comprises entries for 332 archival sources held in the NAI and 68 in PRONI.[11] Sorted by geographical area, it is reproduced in the appendices to this guide and is also available for download in spreadsheet form at http://www.ucd.ie/research/people/business/databaseacga/. The database will be maintained and updated at that URL address. The business records included in the database are categorized and searchable by:

- catalogue number
- name of the company or organization to which the record relates
- town or area in which the company or organization is or was based
- industry or sector
- date of records
- type of record, and
- other comments (such as, for example, whether the records are on micro-fiche).[12]

Great William O'Brien Street, Blackpool, Cork, Ireland. Telephone: +353 (0)21 4505886, Fax: +353 (0)21 4505887, E-mail: archivist@corkcity.ie. For details of opening hours, access and frequently asked questions, see http://www.corkarchives.ie/. **6** Cullen, 'The Irish Manuscripts Commission survey of business records', p. 85. **7** NAI, WAT33. **8** NAI, OFF17. **9** The IAET was established in 1981. Its role is to provide grants for accountancy related research and other relevant projects which would 'further and develop the science of accountancy in all its branches and promote educational facilities for the teaching of accountancy, auditing, finance and other related subjects'. For details on grant applications, see http://www.charteredaccountants.ie/General/About-Us/Irish-Accountancy-Educational-Trust-IAET/ or e-mail iaet@icai.ie **10** Since 1984, *Irish Economic & Social History* has published an annual 'archives report' from the NAI (entitled 'Survey of business records') and the PRONI has produced *Recent accessions of interest to the social and economic historian* (Belfast, various dates). **11** Interestingly, if perhaps counter-intuitively given the industrial prominence of Northern Ireland in historical terms, the PRONI archives featured in this database include less corporate archives than the NAI and a greater number of estate papers and records relating to the voluntary sector. This may be due to the nature of PRONI as an archive; it may also reflect the timeframe for the accessions listed in the database. **12** Given that there are 7 categories and 332 archival sources at the NAI and 68 at the PRONI, this potentially represents 2,324 and 476 pieces of data relating to the NAI and PRONI

The adoption of these different categories allows a researcher to search the segmented data in a variety of ways and at a range of levels. For instance, in some companies or organizations the industry sector will be dispersed nationally, whereas in other cases industry sectors (for example, shipbuilding, milling and linen) may be concentrated in particular geographical areas. Hence, these will be of specific interest to a local historian for whom the facility to sort the database by town or area and/or by catalogue number is especially useful.[13] The business records featured in the database comprise original account books such as accounts ledgers, minute books, correspondence, financial statements and annual reports as well as visitors' books and other operational records (payroll and costing information). In some cases, the account books include cash books and debtors and creditors ledgers. These provide information about the cash receipts and payments of the business as well as individual debtor and creditor balances. Chapter 3 explores a number of potentially viable fields for the study of businesses in local contexts which may draw upon these sources.

GUIDES TO COUNTY SOURCES

PRONI's series of guides to county sources covers all of Ulster and features specific references to a variety of businesses in the northern counties. (While PRONI is the official archive for Northern Ireland, guides have been produced for counties Cavan, Monaghan and Donegal.) For example, PRONI's *Guide to Armagh* includes reference to several sources for the history of the linen industry: for the years 1885 to 1966, a file for the Lurgan Hemmers', Veiners' and General Workers' Union (COM. 76/1/18) is listed and for the period 1909–63 files on Portadown, Banbridge and District Textile Workers' Trade Union are cited (Com. 76/1/27).[14] These guides also offer very useful advice to researchers working with business records at local level. Historians are reminded that a range of sources for business records ought to be considered and consulted. For example, because PRONI collects records from solicitors' offices, the author of the *Guide to Armagh* emphasizes that clients' papers are 'of particular interest to genealogists and local historians as they include records of prominent families, [they invariably kept accounts] landowners and estates – title deeds, testamentary papers, leases, rentals, maps and correspondence, which bring together a corpus of information on a particular family or area.'[15] To demonstrate their usefulness, the records of Carleton, Atkinson & Sloan, a firm of Portadown solicitors, which include the legal papers of the Woodhouse family of Portadown (1850–1912) and the Land Commission papers of the Blacker estate at Carrickblacker, County Armagh, are cited. Armagh Urban District Council solicitors' records (1820–1934) and the records of Watson & Neill,

respectively. **13** For example, material from Dublin is catalogued as DUB, Carlow as CAR, Wicklow as WICK and so on. **14** See PRONI, *Guide to Armagh* (Belfast, 1996), p. 28. **15** Ibid., p. 221.

a firm of Lurgan-based solicitors, relating to Lord Lurgan, are an immensely rich source of information on business activity in that area.

The PRONI *Guide to Armagh* lists the records of the Portadown and Lurgan manufacturing and railway businesses which constitute the 'largest collections of business records' for these towns. These include the business records for the Portadown Gaslight and Electricity Co. Ltd (1859–1974), the minute book of the Portadown Market Co. (1829–1947), as well as records for Portadown Linen Co. (1842–77) and for Bessbrook Spinning Co. (1776–1950). The range of business archives itemized in these guides is evident from a cursory glance at the following entries in the PRONI *Guide to Armagh* (pp 221, 224, 225 and 232):

- 1667–1937: Corr & O'Connor, solicitors, Armagh town, includes records of Crossmaglen Market Society, 1923–7, D.3012
- 1734–1924: Records of Fisher & Fisher, solicitors, includes papers relating to Bessbrook & Newry Tramway Co., D.935.
- 1776–1950: Accounts, letters and other business records and correspondence of the Bessbrook Spinning Co., D.2375/7/5–11.
- 1784–1817: Cash/account book of Richardson's [linen firm], Bessbrook, Co. Armagh, MIC 120/1.
- 1786–92, 1816–1917: Papers of William Hardy Addey, Allistragh, Co. Armagh, power loom manufacturers and finishers, Allistragh Mills, Co. Armagh, D.889/5/2.
- 1795 Linen weavers' cash book, Lurgan area, Co. Armagh, D.1763/1.
- 1806–18: Sales ledger of Thomas C. Atkinson, linen merchant re. sales in British industrial cities, Manchester, Liverpool, Edinburgh, London etc., D.1253/2/2A.
- 1828–29: Account book of grocery business, Loughgall area, Co. Armagh, D.801/3A–B.
- 1829–48: General account book containing list of shareholders and minutes of meetings of shareholders, Tandragee grain store, Co. Armagh, D.1248/X/8.
- 1835–1947: Cash books, day books and accounts of Thomas McLaughlin, auctioneer, Armagh city, D.1709/1–7.
- 1842–77: Records relating to Portadown Linen Co., D.1252/18/1.
- 1847–1946: Diaries, day books, insurance ledger and marine books of J.C. Boyle, estate agent, Armagh, D. 1670.
- 1854–75: 4 volumes relating to the work of the mill on the Brownlow estate, Lurgan, Co. Armagh, D. 1928/M/1–4.
- 1947–50: Industrial development files relating to firms in Co. Armagh applying for grants to the Ministry of Agriculture, COM. 63/1.

This level of specific information is duplicated elsewhere in PRONI's guides for the other eight counties of Ulster. The value of these PRONI *Guides*, which provide such comprehensive lists of available source material, cannot, therefore, be overestimated.

PRONI has also been very active in compiling extensive collections of primary sources for every county in Ulster which may be consulted in its research room and, in many instances, copies may be purchased. In addition, PRONI has compiled a very useful fact sheet on business records for the genealogist or family historian as although many businesses were owned and run by families, this unexpected route to family history has been underutilized. In their collection of business records, not surprisingly, linen, shipbuilding and engineering predominate, ranging from the massive Harland & Wolff to local sole traders. More than 250 companies are represented in the linen industry. As the PRONI research sheets for family historians makes clear, business records 'often contain a great deal of detailed information relating to suppliers, customers and, of course, company employees'. Wage books contain valuable biographical information for a local historian in pursuit of particular individuals. These may include names, addresses, ages, wages and hours worked. Minute books feature material on company affairs, including directors, trustees and how their work affected the local environment. Annual reports of companies may name shareholders. Records of professionals, such as accountants and solicitors, often contain business material, for example, leases and wills: this prompted PRONI to produce a fact sheet on solicitors' records.[16]

In addition to the collections in the island's two major repositories, dedicated professional archives such as those of the Institute of Chartered Accountants (Chartered Accountants' House, Pembroke Road, Dublin 4) can also hold material that is relevant to local studies. Since the early locale of the accounting profession was urban, based particularly in Dublin and Belfast, accountants' archives are likely to be most useful to historians of urban centres. Researchers should also be aware that professional archives are generally catalogued by date.[17]

SOURCES AND THEIR USES IN LOCAL HISTORY

This section identifies the main business sources available to local historians, namely landed estate papers, business directories, dedicated professional archives, ledger accounts, builders' archives, newspapers, solicitors' papers and legal reports, and other business sources.

---

16 PRONI, Your family tree. 18. Business records; Your family tree. Solicitors records. 19. **17** For the ICAI archives, a useful catalogue is available in the ICAI library as *Archive project – exhibition catalogue* (Dublin, 2003). We are grateful to Gerard Reilly (ICAI Librarian) for a copy of this catalogue. The Institute of Chartered Accountants in Ireland has offices in Dublin and Belfast. Contact details: 11 Donegall Square South, Belfast BT1 5JE, Tel: (028) 90321600, Fax: (028) 9023 0071, Contact: Lyndsey McMordie; CA House, 83 Pembroke Road, Ballsbridge, Dublin 4, Tel: (01) 637 7228, Fax: (01) 668 0842 Contact: RIS@icai.ie

Landed estate papers

Leslie A. Clarkson suggests that

> Conspicuous consumption can take many forms. Most tangibly there were
> the building projects – houses and estate villages – that remain visible fea-
> tures of the Irish landscape to this day. It does not stretch categories too far
> to regard the expenditure on these as capital rather than consumption since
> successful estate villages promoted commerce, and country houses func-
> tioned almost like small industries.[18]

Terence Dooley (2000, 2007), Toby Barnard (2005) and others have perceptively
studied patterns of consumption based on evidence contained in the papers of
Ireland's landed estates.[19] For a local historian these can also be an important source
of information concerning the commercial and social life of a local or estate community. For instance, Peter Clarke has highlighted how the accounts produced for
the earl of Norfolk between 1279 and 1294 for his estates in Carlow and Wexford
'throw a remarkable light on the Middle Ages, since they give minute details of the
sales of cattle and crops, wages, and the cost of buildings and repairs.'[20] We get a
glimpse of the range of material available to historians in the work of Leslie
Clarkson.[21] He has drawn upon the account books of the following: the Balfour
family at Townley Hall in Drogheda;[22] the Plunkett family, earls of Fingal, in
County Meath (1780s and 1790s);[23] Thomas Conolly, Castletown, County Kildare
(which record the largest expenditure of all records consulted);[24] the households of
the bishops of Down and Connor;[25] the Carew family, County Waterford;[26]
Mathew Weekes, steward of the earl of Inchiquin in County Clare,[27] and the

18 Leslie Clarkson, 'Hospitality, housekeeping and high living in eighteenth-century
Ireland' in J.R. Hill and Colm Lennon (eds), *Luxury and austerity: Historical Studies, XXI*
(Dublin, 1999), pp 85–6.   19 See Terence A.M. Dooley, *Sources for the history of landed estates*
(Dublin, 2000); idem, *The big houses and landed estates of Ireland: a research guide* (Dublin,
2007); Toby Barnard, *A guide to the sources for material culture in Ireland, 1500–2000* (Dublin,
2005).   20 Peter Clarke, 'The historical evolution of accounting practice in Ireland' in *The
Irish Accounting Review*, 13 (Spring 2006), pp 1–23: p. 2. These records are included in
Richard Hayes's *Manuscript sources for the history of Irish civilization* (11 vols, Boston, MA,
1966) and *Manuscript sources for the history of Irish civilization. First supplement, 1965–75* (3 vols,
Boston, MA, 1979).   21 Cullen, 'The Irish Manuscripts Commission survey of business
records', p. 86.   22 Household accounts of the Balfours of Townley Hall, Drogheda, 1812–
16 (NLI, MS 11901).   23 Household accounts of the Plunkett family, earls of Fingal,
County Meath, 1781–99 (NLI, MS 8038, 5–11).   24 Household accounts of the Conolly
family, Castletown, County Kildare, 1783–7 (PRONI, Mic. 435) and Household accounts
of the Conolly family, Castletown, County Kildare, 1828 (NLI, MS 14342).   25 Account
book of Edward Pierce, steward of Thomas Hackett, bishop of Down and Connor, 1674
(PRONI, DIO/26/1) and account book of Francis Hutchinson, bishop of Down and
Connor, 1729–34 (PRONI, DIO/22/1).   26 Accounts of Carew family, County
Waterford, 1738–82 in *Shapland Carew papers*, ed. A.K. Longfield (Dublin, 1946).   27 Daily
account book of Mathew Weekes, steward of the earl of Inchiquin, County Clare, 1746

Aldercon family.[28] Furthermore, in the course of her study of rural society in post-Cromwellian Ireland, Margaret MacCurtain highlighted the importance of the scholarship of David Lodge who demonstrated the value of rents and rental books in deepening our understanding of the financial and business activities of landowners.[29] More generally, the rapidly expanding corpus of scholarly studies of landed estates in early modern and modern Ireland provides local historians researching particular estates with valuable leads to collections of landowners' records held in both public and private custody.

Business directories

Business directories which are available for consultation in the National Library of Ireland on Kildare Street, Dublin 2 and in other major libraries, are an important but largely untapped source of historical information for the local historian, revealing a wealth of information ranging from the numbers of silversmiths to the credit ratings of prominent individuals such as Republican, Theobald Wolfe Tone, who features in the accounts of the Bank of Ireland lodged in the Gilbert Library, Pearse Street, Dublin 2. Richard Lucas's *The Cork Directory for the year 1787* features lists of merchants and traders for Cork city (pp 9–56), Cove (p. 60), Passage (p. 60), Innishannon (p. 60), Kinsale (p. 62), Bandon (p. 64) and Youghal (p. 69). These lists give addresses of businesses in the area, their hours of business as well as their trade/occupation/profession. The businesses are listed in alphabetical order. We also can form a picture of the professional cadre in Cork from the lists of barristers-at-law (pp 56–7), physicians and surgeons (pp 57–8) whose names and addresses are recorded. Based on all of these lists combined, the level of business activity of Cork and its hinterland in the late eighteenth century can be assessed.

A number of similar directories exist for different periods and for different counties. The Gilbert Library, Pearse Street, Dublin 2, holds microfiche copies of several volumes of Pigot's Directory (1820, 1821, 1822 and 1824), the earliest directories in the collection to cover the whole of Ireland, as well as copies of Slater's Directory of Ireland (1846, 1856, 1870, 1881 and 1894).[30] The 1894 edition of Slater's Directory has a general directory of private residents of Ireland which is especially useful for local historians. Other directories in the Gilbert Library collection which

(NLI, MS 11909).   **28** Weekly food purchases of the Aldercon family, 1785–6 (NLI, MS 3846).   **29** Margaret MacCurtain, 'Rural society in post-Cromwellian Ireland' in Art Cosgrove and Donal McCartney (eds), *Studies in Irish history* (Naas, 1979), pp 118–36: p. 136; David Lodge, 'The wealth of the greater Irish landowners, 1750–1815' in *Irish Historical Studies*, 15:57 (Mar. 1966), p. 25.   **30** For more information on directories in the Gilbert collection, see http://www.dublincity.ie/RECREATIONANDCULTURE/LIBRARIES/HERITAGE%20AND%20HISTORY/COLLECTIONS/Pages/directories.aspx. As noted on this site, 'an almost complete set of Dublin directories from 1751 to the present is held in hardcopy in the Gilbert Library: Wilson's Dublin Directories 1751–3 … 1761–1837; Pettigrew and Oulton's Dublin Directories 1837–47; Thom's Irish Almanac and Official Directories 1844–present. These early directories, from 1751 to 1833, are in surname order only. From 1834, street listings are available as well as the name sequence.'

cover counties apart from Dublin include Bassett's directories of Wexford (1885), Down (1886) and Tipperary (1889); Gillespie's *Co. Monaghan Directory and Almanac* (1892); Griffith's *County Wexford Almanac* (1874); Egan's *History, Guide and Directory of County and City of Waterford* (1892); Lowe's *County Fermanagh Directory and Household Almanac* (1880) and Francis Guy's *Directory of Munster* (1886). Belfast and Ulster directories are available for 1924, 1930, 1934 and 1940, and copies of Belfast and Northern Ireland directories for the years 1941, 1951–62, 1964, 1966–72, 1979, 1914 and 1996, which include street listings for Belfast, also feature in the library's holdings.

Ledgers, account books and credit ratings

The Gilbert Library has a ledger entitled 'Bank Stock 1783–1801' which records revealing information on credit ratings and other comments on clients of the bank. The files contain alphabetical lists of names, addresses, on occasion, occupation and other details of customers holding Bank of Ireland accounts including, for example, James Flemming, a grazier from Boardstown, County Cork and members of the La Touche banking family of County Kildare. Although the entries are not arranged in geographical order, it is none the less possible to locate files for particular individuals or families who were Bank of Ireland customers in this period. Another informative source found in these files is Wilson's *Dublin Directory with additions. 1789–*. The copy in the Bank Stock archives belonged to the Bank of Ireland and appears to have been used as a source of credit rating information. This directory is replete with individual credit ratings and comments such as 'Alley, George and Peter, grocers, 79 Kevin Street, "broke"' (p. 14); 'Ashmore, Richard, woollen-draper, 21 Francis Street, "broke"' (p. 15); 'Bulkely, Edward, agent, 53 Great Britain Street', with a comment added 'agent to the Right Hon. Thomas Connolly [*sic.*]' (p. 21); 'Ford, Alice, thread and tape manufacturer, 50 Thomas Street, "her husband lives abroad"' (p. 40) and alongside the entry for Robert Shuter, linen draper, 23 King Street, a note to 'be cautious of Pat Murphy's bills on Shuter from Drogheda' (p. 81).

Builders' and builders' suppliers archives

Builders' archives can also contain information of relevance to local historians wishing to trace the early history of a particular building, including details about when it was originally built, extended, renovated and so on. Collections contain operational and administrative records. While the survival rate of builders' archives is low and the level of detail varies, they can provide good evidence of the built landscape of a local area. For example, the files of Timothy Naughton, a member of a well-known Galway family of merchants and builders' suppliers, include a bill from James Stewart, a well-known Galway builder, dated 20 August 1906 for cement work completed at Newcastle Lodge. In the same file and at the other end of the scale is a bill from J. Eustace, Church House, 63 Lower Salthill, Galway for the sum of 12 shillings for a picture rail.[31] A limited number of builders files, classed as business archives, are available for consultation in the NAI. See appendix 1 for some builders' archives, for instance, Cooney Jennings Ltd (DUB 156 in the NAI), Thomas Williamson Ltd (LOU 15 in the NAI), Rileys and Boland of Ballina (MAYO 20 in the NAI), and James Buckley & Sons of Belfast (D.3900 in PRONI).

Local and national newspapers

Local and national newspapers can serve as exceptionally revealing sources on the array of businesses operating in Ireland from the eighteenth century onwards, when provincial newspaper publishing became widespread.[32] In her 1998 article, which contains a wealth of information on provincial newspapers in Munster and South Leinster, Máire Kennedy states that the towns of that region had a stable newspaper publishing regime in operation from the mid-eighteenth century. In Limerick this dates from 1739, in Cork from 1753, in Waterford (1765), Kilkenny (1766), followed by Clonmel (1772), Tralee (1774) and Ennis (1778). These newspapers offer unique information on business activity at local level and provide indications of the range of business contacts and partnerships that existed in specific regions throughout the country.[33] Surviving issues of Irish newspapers are listed in O'Toole's joint 1992 National Library of Ireland and British Library publication *Newsplan: report of the Newsplan project in Ireland* which is available in the National Library of Ireland and other major libraries.

Newspapers are especially valuable sources for researchers studying the past business and commercial life of a local community. They carry accounts of and/or advertisements for trading events such as auctions, supply of services, marts and markets and business openings and closures. As such they can be an important source for dating particular events that occurred within a local community or for shedding light on the public perspective on, or knowledge of, individual transactions or events that transpired in a village or town. More specifically, reports on market prices, court proceedings and shipping news can contain valuable information on the business and commercial life of a local community. Similarly, reports on social events such as race meetings, theatrical reviews and contributions in poetry and prose by local residents also serve as a lens through which the social life of a local community can be viewed.

Advertisements are especially illuminating in respect of local businesses. They can vary in both content and context: in the eighteenth century, advertisements were generally placed by 'prosperous businesses, especially those dealing in luxury commodities: wine and spirits, drapery and millinery, books and periodicals, patent medicines, garden plants and seeds and other luxury foods'.[34] Hence, they are indicative of levels of prosperity and consumption within a local community.

31 NAI, GAL 3/5. **32** Máire Kennedy, 'Eighteenth-century newspaper publishing in Munster and South Leinster' in *Journal of the Cork Historical and Archaeological Society*, 103 (1998), pp 67–8: p. 67. **33** Ibid., p. 68. **34** Ibid., p. 77.

However, with the expansion of middle-class consumption in the nineteenth century, advertising extended to embrace consumer and household goods in general.
Advertisements therefore provide useful information on suppliers and on the types
of businesses operating in a given locality whilst also reflecting changing patterns of
consumption. Furthermore, an analysis of newspaper notices allows scope for ascer-
taining how and to what extent local business communities interacted with the
State. For example, in July 1805 the *General Advertiser and Limerick Gazette* printed
a letter issued from Dublin Castle stating that the Lord Lieutenant 'would be
pleased to order a supply of the new silver coinage to be sent to the collector in
Limerick.'[35] More generally, newspapers were significant agents in shaping public
opinion and public tastes from the late eighteenth century onwards. In short, newspapers serve as a vitally important window on business and commercial activity
within local communities across Ireland from the mid-eighteenth and more especially the early nineteenth century onwards. While the National Library of Ireland
holds the largest collection of Irish national and provincial newspapers in both hard
and microform copies, researchers may also access newspapers in other repositories
such as the Gilbert Library, Pearse Street, Dublin 2, or their county library or, alter-
natively, the office of the newspaper if it is still circulated.

Furthermore, the records of complimentary areas of business, such as printers,
can also be a source of revealing information about the life of a local community.
The names and addresses of printers may be found in the business directories discussed above and their records are stored in various archives including the NAI,
PRONI and the NLI. For example, the archives of one printer, Christopher
Taylor of Wexford,[36] reveal a great deal about the experiences of his local community during the crisis of the 1798 rebellion.

Solicitors' papers and legal reports

In general, solicitors' papers and legal reports contain fascinating material on leases
and other forms of agreement – or disagreement – which can be usefully mined by
business and local historians. For example, Anthony Malcomson's work tracing
'perhaps the longest running and most celebrated lawsuits' in Ireland – known generally as Loftus v. Hume – charts the struggle of successive Lords Ely over their
entitlement to the estates of the Hume family in counties Fermanagh (Castle
Hume), Leitrim (Manorhamilton), Kildare (Monasterevin), Mayo and Wexford
(New Ross).[37] As a source for local historians in these areas, such macro-level
machinations cast light on micro-level histories.

---

35 *General Advertiser and Limerick Gazette*, 29 July 1805.   **36** See the papers of Christopher
Taylor, Wexford printer, in Prints section, NLI. We are grateful to Colette O'Daly for
alerting us to this source. Taylor printed for the militia, yeomanry and the rebels, as well as
for a whole range of businesses.   **37** A.P.W. Malcomson, 'A house divided: the Loftus
family, earls and marquesses of Ely, *c.*1600–*c.*1900' in David Dickson and Cormac Ó Gráda
(eds), *Refiguring Ireland. Essays in honour of L.M. Cullen* (Dublin, 2003), pp 184–224.

Other business sources

Local historians should also be aware of the sometimes serendipitous value of other archival sources for the study of business and commercial life in their chosen community. It is worth noting that a resourceful approach to archival collections and a consideration of creative, lateral avenues of research can bring rewards. For example, as will be discussed later, files archived as the private ledger of the Sweeney brothers, solicitors, includes documentation from Hibernian Bank and A.D. Comyn, solicitors, both in Loughrea, and also Ballinasloe Garage.[38] The garage records include a long list of names under the heading 'Bad debts accumulated', including the Revd Keenan PP of Ballymacurand, who owed 2*s*. Hotel visitors' books are also fascinating sources for local historians with an interest in the business and in visitors to a locality. For example, the business records of Glynn's hotel in Gort, County Galway include the visitors' book which covers the period 1947 to 1952. In their entries visitors from Ireland, England and the United States recounted where they have been and where they planned to visit.[39] For the student of tourism in the west, this is an invaluable source which testifies to the cosmopolitanism of certain local communities in twentieth-century Ireland.

Local historians should also be aware of business archives held in private hands: these are evidently more sporadic in nature and beyond the scope of this book. However, examples of the good use of such less-accessible archives can be found in the work of Miriam Lambe and Jim Gilligan.[40] These articles make use of archives in the hands of Matthew Stapleton, Borrisoleigh, County Tipperary and Brendan Murray, Dunshaughlin, County Meath respectively to develop microstudies of local business and their impact on the towns in which they are located and are invitations to emulation to others who can access such archives – and an encouragement to others who hold such archives to make them more widely available by depositing them in public archives such as the NAI or PRONI. (See Table 6 in chapter 3 for examples of grocers and merchants archives in the NAI.)

This chapter has presented an overview of those business archives held in the NAI and PRONI which are the most voluminous and most wide-ranging collections likely to be of interest and use to local historians, together with details of the main guides, surveys and categories of source material. In order to enable a researcher to find sources that have particular relevance to his or her chosen locality, the collections in these two repositories are listed in an EXCEL spreadsheet (see appendices 1 & 2) which can be downloaded and sorted by area. The next chapter examines in greater detail the potential use of these archival sources for local studies.

38 NAI, GAL 2/1/1.   **39** NAI, GAL 8/1.   **40** Miriam Lambe, 'At the Cross: a shop in rural Ireland, 1880–1911' in Denis A. Cronin, Jim Gilligan and Karina Holton (eds), *Irish fairs and markets: studies in local history* (Dublin, 2001), pp 206–23. Jim Gilligan, 'Murray's of Dunshaughlin, 1896–1910' in Cronin, Gilligan & Holton (eds), *Irish fairs and markets*, pp 224–48.

CHAPTER 3

Potential uses of business archival sources for the local historian

Along with Church and government/official records, businessmen and women documented the commercial life of their communities, recording transactions and events at grassroots level as well as developments that connected their locality with the wider world.[1] Businesses were settings for socialization, employment, exchange of goods and services, consumption and accommodation and consequently their archival legacy contains a wealth of often mundane detail which allows researchers to reconstruct a picture of what life was like in a local community in the past. This chapter therefore presents a number of examples of how business archives, particularly those detailed in this guide, may be used by a local historian. Whilst the primary value of these archival collections is as sources of information regarding the history of one or more businesses or even of an entire industry or sector, when used imaginatively these records can also offer insights into the economic and social life of the wider communities in which they were located and with which they engaged. As such they serve as a lens through which more general social and economic changes wrought upon those communities may be analysed and assessed. Examples of the potential use of business sources in illuminating these wider trends are therefore discussed and a selection of case histories illustrating the use of accounting and business archives for local studies are very briefly outlined.

SOURCES FOR THE HISTORY OF LOCAL BUSINESSES

Organizational histories

As indicated in chapter one, a modest number of organizational histories have been published. However, several large organizations whose records are available have yet to be afforded scholarly attention. These include Telecom Éireann whose administrative and operational records, maps, plans and drawings span the period 1870 to 1995 (NAI, 2001/95); the Irish Mining Company whose records comprise cash books, ledgers, sales and purchases books, as well as wages books covering the years 1885 to 1969 (NAI, DUB 64); Winstanley Ltd, a shoe manufacturer in Dublin

---

1 Raymond Refaussé, *Church of Ireland records* (Dublin, 2000; 2nd ed., 2006); Patrick J. Corish and David C. Sheehy, *Records of the Irish Catholic Church* (Dublin, 2001); Brian Griffin, *Sources for the study of crime in Ireland, 1801–1921* (Dublin, 2005).

whose accounts, operational books and files are available for the period from 1930 to 1980 (NAI, DUB 81), and The Gaiety Theatre Co. Ltd (NAI, DUB 144) whose administrative records date from the early twentieth century. Other major archival collections include the registers and daily lists of the Dublin Stock Exchange from 1802 to 1961 (NAI, DUB 77; see also Thomas (1986) for a history of the stock exchanges in Ireland). Banks and bank records are also a revealing lens through which networks of family and professional contacts based upon financial arrangements can be examined. In his study of the role of landlords, bankers and merchants in Ireland's emerging banking sector, Louis Cullen draws upon the La Touche and Kane ledgers in the NLI and suggests that 'from its foundation in 1719 the bank of La Touche and Kane operated what was virtually a country-wide system of correspondents'. Emphasizing the importance of landlords in providing an impetus to the development of banking in Ireland, he forefronts a number of banking families and their foundations at local level in his study, namely the Hoares of Cork, Cairnes in Limerick ('the only known provincial "branch" of a Dublin bank in the eighteenth century'), the Colcloughs of Wexford, Talbot at Malahide, the ffrenchs at Tuam and the Langrishes in Kilkenny. Encouragingly Cullen alerts historians to the fact that 'before the 1760s Irish banking was more interesting than Scottish: [having] a larger circulation of notes, more numerous locations and the outline of a national credit structure'. He goes on to suggest that the abstract ledger of La Touche and Kane (1726–43), Allied Irish Banks, Dublin, would provide researchers with information necessary for undertaking such a study.[2] The Bank of Ireland, which was established in 1783, has an official history which is a mine of information on various banking activities covering two hundred years. Of particular interest is T.K. Whitaker's opening chapter on the origins and consolidation of the bank which details the La Touche family's involvement in the development of the institution. David La Touche was the first governor of the bank. Whitaker (formerly permanent secretary at the Department of Finance) outlines the historical context for the formation of this significant business institution which, like other banks, contributed to the development of Ireland's major cities.[3] Hence, there is considerable scope for assessing the role of business activity at grassroots level outside of the capital through analysis of banking records.

These institutions frequently employed substantial numbers of staff and, fortunately, the Irish Bank Officials' Association has catalogued its archives. Over 2,000 items in the archive have been summarized in a database compiled by labour historian, Tom Crean.[4] A hard copy of the database is available for consultation in the Irish Labour History Society Library, Beggars Bush, Haddington Road, Dublin 4.[5]

2 W.A. Thomas, *The stock exchanges of Ireland* (Dublin, 1986); L.M. Cullen, 'Landlords, bankers and merchants: the early Irish banking world, 1700–1820' in Antoin Murphy (ed.), *Economists and the Irish economy from the eighteenth century to the present day* (Dublin, 1984) pp 25–44: pp 27, 43. 3 T.K. Whitaker, 'Origins and consolidation, 1783–1826' in F.S.L. Lyons (ed.), *Bank of Ireland: bicentenary essays* (Dublin, 1983), pp 11–29. 4 Tom Crean, 'The reorganisation of the records of the Irish Bank Officials' Association' in *Saothar*, 27 (2002), pp 112–13. 5 Opening hours: Monday–Friday 10:00–13:00. Access is by prior appointment only. Phone or Fax: +353 (0)1 6681071.

1 On the corner of Nassau Street and Grafton Street, *c.*1900, Clarke (?) 26,
courtesy of the National Library of Ireland

2 Quiet Dalkey streetscape with medical hall (pharmacy), Niall Murphy, 1904,
postcard collection, courtesy of the National Library of Ireland

3 Last Hill of Howth tram, INDR 2238, courtesy of the National Library
of Ireland

4 Busy Grafton Street, Dublin *c.*1880, Praeger Collection © Royal Irish
Academy

A *Select guide to trade union records in Dublin*, edited by Sarah Ward-Perkins, which surveys trade union records in union premises and institutions in Dublin, is another invaluable reference book, providing outline histories, membership figures and descriptions of the records for 128 unions, as well as listing over 950 trade societies and unions which operated in Ireland until approximately 1970.[6] Thanks to the work of Mary Clark and Raymond Refaussé, who have made available the extensive records of Dublin guilds, growing familiarity with these archival sources has opened new research avenues for historians in general.[7] Terence Dooley's published guides to sources for the history of Big Houses and landed estates have had a similar effect on scholarly research and publication.[8]

In addition, there was a very long tradition of Quaker involvement in Irish industry, particularly milling. As Cullen notes for the eighteenth century, the 'Quakers were a distinctive group even within dissenters in Dublin, usually drawing on provincial families for their growth. Thus Pikes from Cork, Clibborns, Strettells, Pims, Bewleys and Strangmans from the midlands were prominent as were more Dublin-based families such as Fades, Willcox, Forbes, and Jaffrays.'[9] The Quaker archives in Stocking Lane, Rathfarnham, Dublin 16 are an excellent source for information on the history of the Quakers and Quaker families. The documents in these archives include title deeds and minute books of meetings throughout Ireland together with letters, wills, photographs and other personal material.[10]

Sectoral histories

Sectoral histories have long been the staple diet of business and accounting historians. Given that particular industrial sectors in Ireland were relatively localized – for example, shipbuilding in the northeast, milling in the southeast and midlands – there are strong sectoral and local connections which may also be exploited by the local historian. The potential for research and publication of such sectoral histories can be seen from examining table 1 which sets out a number of sectors or industries and details of companies whose records are held in the NAI or in the PRONI. Similarly, the list of business records featured in appendices 1 and 2 enables researchers to identify at a glance specific sectors or industries and the corresponding archival collections.

---

6 Sarah Ward-Perkins (ed.), *Select guide to trade union records in Dublin* (Dublin, 1996). 7 Mary Clark and Raymond Refaussé (eds), *Directory of historic Dublin guilds* (Dublin, 1993). 8 Dooley, *Sources for the history of landed estates in Ireland*; idem, *The big house and landed estates of Ireland: a research guide*. 9 L.M. Cullen, 'The Dublin merchant community of the eighteenth century' in Paul Butel and L.M. Cullen (eds), *Cities and merchants: French and Irish perspectives on urban development, 1500–1900* (Dublin, 1986), pp 195–209: pp 200–1. 10 See http://www.quakers-in-ireland.ie/archive/indexarc.htm for opening hours, contact details and an index of printed material in these archives. Enquiries regarding Quaker archives and records for Ulster should be addressed to Ulster Quarterly Meeting Archives Committee, 4 Magheralave Road, Lisburn, BT28 3BD.

Table 1: Examples of records spanning changes at the turn of the twentieth century

Catalogue number	Name of organization or company	Industry or sector	Area	Date	Type of record
DUB 79	Fannin and Co.	Surgical instrument makers	Dublin	1867–1971	minute books, audited accounts
DUB 75	Donnelly (Dublin) Ltd	Bacon factors	Dublin	1880–1980	minute books, account books, deeds and leases
WAT 30	Clyde Shipping Co.	Shipping	Waterford	1889–1975	wages books, operational books and files
★★	Switzer & Co.	Retail	Dublin	1890–	account books, minute books
DUB 64	Irish Mining Company	Mining	Dublin	1885–1969	cash books, ledgers, sales and purchases books, wages books

Source: Drawn from Ó hÓgartaigh & Ó hÓgartaigh, Database of Corporate Governance Archives, http://www.ucd.ie/research/people/business/databaseacga/

The available archival collections provide very considerable scope for sectoral studies at local community level: studies of this kind have been completed in the past by L.M. Cullen and Akihiro Takei,[11] although few, if any, have been undertaken with a specific focus on accounting. Various forms of milling are particularly well represented among surviving archival collections, with the NAI holding material relating to large mills (Odlum's, Ranks and Boland's Mills) and small ones (for instance, Malcolmson's of Waterford and Morrin's of Wicklow), incorporated mills (for example, Celbridge [carpet] Mills Ltd) and family-owned businesses such as Cloney's, the Fogarty family's Aughrim Mill, and the Clara and Belmont Mills which were owned by the Perry family. As well as pointing to potential contrasts in governance practices between mills, these archives also hold records for groups of mills, allowing a study of relationships and pricing practices between associated mills. For example, the records of Odlum Limited (from 1881) include those of Odlums (Sallins) Ltd, W.P. & R. Odlum Ltd, Dublin Port Milling Co. Ltd, National Flour Mills Ltd, Irish Grain Ltd, Procea Ltd, Johnson, Mooney and O'Brien Ltd, Dublin Silo Co. Ltd, Euroglas Ltd, and W. & G.T. Pollexfen[12] and Co. Ltd. In addition to studies of relationships within business organizations, there

11 L.M. Cullen, 'Eighteenth-century flour milling in Ireland' in *Irish Economic & Social History*, 4 (1997), pp 5–25; Akihiro Takei, 'The first Irish linen mills – 1800–1824' in *Irish Economic & Social History*, 21 (1994), pp 28–38. **12** The Pollexfens were W.B. Yeats's maternal ancestors.

is potential for examining relationships between businesses based on the records of millers, maltsers (such as Egan Tarleton of Tullamore, County Offaly) and grain merchants (for instance, R. & H. Hall's mills in Dublin, Cork and Waterford). On another level, interesting customer perspectives can also be gleaned from the records of Dublin and Alliance Gas and the Consumers' Association which are held in the NAI.[13]

BUSINESS SOURCES IN A WIDER CONTEXT

This section explores the potential use of business sources in developing an understanding of several aspects of a local community's history. The examples featured here are not intended to be exhaustive; rather they are suggested ways in which historians might profitably engage with business archives. Businesses, as recorders of economic (and other) transactions and events, have bequeathed to the historian a particular perspective on 'getting and spending' in their local community.[14] Given that businesses 'were locales of consumption, business records represent a realm of social action, interaction and experience which increasingly structures the everyday practices of urban [and rural] people'.[15] Scholarly studies of the role of business in the wider development of urban communities have proved particularly illuminating. In his careful examination of the merchant community of Waterford in the sixteenth and seventeenth centuries, Julian Walton explains that while there are 'no notarial archives and account book or correspondence detailing the trade of individual firms', corporation records and the reports of merchants, who conducted business in France and Spain, can rectify these archival deficits. He also suggests that local historians can profit from using court pleadings as well as the extensive corporation manuscripts published by the Irish Manuscripts Commission.[16] Walton illustrates his point by directing historians' attention to the 'many references [made] in the State papers to the problems of arresting, imprisoning and dispatching the culprits to Dublin and ... obtaining compensation for goods lost. Furthermore, the municipal statutes include information on wool, sheepskins, tallow, butter and salted meat.'[17] L.M. Cullen's careful analysis of the Dublin merchant community in the eighteenth century reveals interesting links between this élite and government and politics in general, demonstrating that commercial life frequently mirrored political changes. Cullen provides useful figures on the growth of various business classes between 1751 and 1799 and suggests that 'it is not surprising that provincial

13 NAI, DUB 177.   **14** Leslie A. Clarkson, 'Irish social history, 1974–2000 and beyond' in *Irish Economic & Social History*, 28 (2002), pp 1–12: p. 12.   **15** Pasi Falk and Colin Campbell, *The shopping experience* (London, 1997), p. 1.   **16** Julian Walton, 'The merchant community of Waterford in the 16th and 17th centuries' in Butel & Cullen (eds), *Cities and merchants*, pp 183–92: p. 183.   **17** Walton, 'Merchant community of Waterford', p. 184; see also idem, 'The household effects of a Waterford merchant family in 1640' in *Cork Archaeological and Historical Society*, 238 (1978), pp 99–105.

Catholic and dissenter merchants seem to have accelerated their establishment in Dublin' in the mid-eighteenth century 'in line with the rapid expansion of the economy' during that period.[18] As these local studies illustrate, business records can tell a lot about the national economic environment.

It is also possible to gain insights into the state of the economy of western Europe (particularly France in the eighteenth century) through analysis of the business activities and records of certain Irish émigré families; for example, the Creagh family of Limerick was just one of several Irish families who had thriving business interests in Nantes in the eighteenth century.[19] Among the more well-known Irish émigré entrepreneurs on the Continent in the early modern period were the Hennessys of Cork who established a thriving Cognac business in France in 1794. Ciarán Ó hÓgartaigh and Margaret Ó hÓgartaigh have shown that apart from shedding light on their commercial enterprises, the success of those generations of Irish migrants abroad reflects the educational context – at both national and local levels – that obtained in the Ireland they left behind.[20]

Business history as discontinuity: dates or turning points

In their introduction to what they term 'the new accounting history', Peter Miller, Trevor Hopper and Richard Laughlin define no theoretical boundaries within which business research must be based, nor do they set out standard methodologies to which all research must subscribe. Accounting history, they argue, should not be viewed simply as some natural evolution.[21] History – and accounting history in particular – is increasingly seen as a study of discontinuity rather than of evolution and it is recognized that the sources of such discontinuity in business history can be found in legislative or political change as well as in the turbulence of the business and economic climate. The increasing professionalization and regulation of business resulting from such change can initially – if perhaps somewhat simplistically – be periodized in the following manner: firstly, the increased professionalization of the late nineteenth and early twentieth centuries, secondly, the introduction of company legislation in the Republic of Ireland in 1963, and thirdly, amendments to such legislation in 1986 and afterwards. Tables 1 and 2 reproduce selected elements of the database, sorted by date, which highlight the implications that these changes had for reporting entities since these archival sources span the period before and after the introduction of the changes.

18 Cullen, 'Dublin merchant community', p. 197.   **19** Archives départmentales de la Loire Atlantique, Étude Boufflet, Eii 352, 330 Sept. 1735; cited in Cullen, 'Dublin merchant community', p. 208; see also idem, 'Apotheosis and crisis; the Irish diaspora in the age of Choiseul' in Thomas O'Connor and Mary Ann Lyons (eds), *Irish communities in early-modern Europe* (Dublin, 2006) pp 6–31: p. 25.   **20** Richard Hennessy mentioned learning accounting in a Cork hedge school, see Ó hÓgartaigh & Ó hÓgartaigh, 'Teaching accounting in eighteenth-century Ireland'.   **21** Miller et al., 'The new accounting history: an introduction', pp 395–403; Peter Miller and Christopher Napier, 'Genealogies of calculation' in *Accounting, Organizations and Society*, 18 (1993), pp 631–47.

Table 2: Examples of records spanning the introduction of the 1963 Companies Act

Catalogue number	Name of organization or company	Industry or sector	Area	Date	Type of record
DUB 47	John Ireland and Son Ltd	Uniform clothing manufacturers	Dublin	1940–67	accounts
LIM 28	Limerick Shipping Co.	Shipping	Limerick	1940–70	minute books, agenda books, company registers
DUB 129	McCullough Pigott Ltd	Musical instrument dealers	Dublin	1941–	piano sales book, various administrative records

Source: Drawn from Ó hÓgartaigh & Ó hÓgartaigh, Database of Corporate Governance Archives, http://www.ucd.ie/research/people/business/databaseacga/

Table 3: Examples of some sectors replete with records

Industry/sector	Archive	Companies/Organizations
Retailing	NAI	Arnotts, Switzers, McBirneys, Pim Brothers
Grain Milling	NAI	Odlum's, Ranks (Ireland), Boland's Mills, Malcolmson's, Morrin and Son Ltd, Celbridge Mills Ltd, Aughrim Mill (Fogarty family), Cloney's, Clara and Belmont Mills (Perry family), North Dublin Milling Co., Thomas Swan of Buncrana.
Milling	PRONI	Samuel and John Cunningham of Belfast, Moygashel Mills, Braid Water Spinning Mill
Food manufacturers	NAI	W. & C. McDonnell Ltd, Clover Meats Ltd (Wexford and Waterford), Clonmel Foods Ltd, Roscrea Meat Products, Castlebar Bacon Company Ltd
Hospitals	NAI	The Coombe, Mater Misericordiae, Dublin Tuberculosis Hospitals, St John's, Mercer's Hospital, The Rotunda
Pharmacies	NAI	Devlin Medical Hall, Johnston's Pharmacy, Gaskin family, Ardee dispensary
Gas companies	NAI	Waterford Gas Company, Longford Gas Company
Grocers	NAI	27 grocers, merchants and department stores
Bars and hotels	NAI	Mrs Burns' Temperance hotel (Westport), Glynn's hotel (Gort), Leen's hotel (Abbeyfeale)
Linen manufacturers	PRONI	Wolfhill Spinning Co., Ulster Spinning Co., Grove Spinning Co.
Co-operative Societies	PRONI	Belfast Co-operative Society Ltd, Lisburn Co-operative Society Ltd, Irish Co-operative Society Ltd
Solicitors	NAI, PRONI	Charles J. Holohan; John J. Duggan; John Wray and Co.; Goodbody and Kennedy; Maxwell, Weldon & Co.; Margetson and Green
Malsters	NAI	P.J. Roche & Sons (New Ross), Egan Tarleton (Tullamore), Gibney (Port Laoise)

Source: Drawn from Ó hÓgartaigh & Ó hÓgartaigh, Database of Corporate Governance Archives, http://www.ucd.ie/research/people/business/databaseacga/

Table 4: Estate papers in the PRONI

D.3531 add.	Shirley estate	estate	Carrickmacross, Co. Monaghan	1814–1919	accounts, leases, workers' time books
T. 3763; MIC 537	Langford estates	estate	Antrim and Londonderry	1610–1804	accounts, leases, title deeds, rentals
T. 3765	Rawdon estates	estate	Ballynahinch and Moira	c.1630–1781	accounts, rentals, title deeds, tenants' petitions
D. 1928 add.	William Brownlow	estate	Lurgan	1752–1754	estate and household account
D. 2784/23	Downshire estates	estate	Antrim and Down	1744–1930	rent rolls and cash books
D. 2784/23	Deramore estates	estate	Down	1939–1969	cash book
D. 3990		estate	Londonderry	1775–1793	account book
D/4233	Armar Corry	estate	Antrim, Down and Fermanagh	1886–1928	rentals
D/2638	Needham	estate	Newry and Mourne	1821–1920	rentals
D/1503	Earl Annesley	estate	Castlewellan, Co. Down	1813–1918	estate rentals and cashbooks

Source: Drawn from Ó hÓgartaigh & Ó hÓgartaigh, Database of Corporate Governance Archives, http://www.ucd.ie/research/people/business/databaseacga/

The dates or turning points featured here represent changes in the national or macro- economy and regulatory context. Local historians will, of course, be particularly concerned with phases of significant economic change at local level. Industrial or agricultural expansion or decline, changes in ownership or use of estates, factories and other businesses and their potential effects on the local economy, representations of bad debts, trends in employment and economic well-being as well as traces of social change, patterns of migration and shifts in social, economic and physical geography (such as buildings or streetscapes) may be reflected in the archives of local businesses. The reaction of companies and organizations in the face of changes in their environment may in itself be an interesting phenomenon which local historians are well-equipped to interpret through their knowledge of the local context.

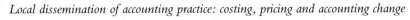

Local dissemination of accounting practice: costing, pricing and accounting change

Some of the more interesting and challenging areas of business history are those which relate, firstly, to the dissemination of changes in accounting practice, following from Hoskin and Macve's seminal study of the influence of military training at West Point on measurement technologies and, secondly, to Foucauldian perspectives of accounting as a means of control. Jeacle and Walsh have applied such perspectives to the development of accounting systems in the retail context.[22] In the NAI and PRONI business records there are rich pickings for local historians working in this area. The nexus of these changes in accounting practices could include individuals, groups or geographical areas and may be evidenced in accounting records such as cost books and debtors ledgers. The archives hold diaries and correspondence of several significant business people such as Professor Pierce Purcell (prominent in the development of the Irish Peat Fuel Industry in the first half of the twentieth century)[23] and Dr Tim O'Driscoll who was involved in the development of both Aer Lingus and Bord Fáilte in the mid-twentieth century.

In the context of local studies, certain areas are particularly well represented (for example, retailers in Westport) as are specific groups of companies (for instance, Odlums). Networks of relationships and patterns of exchange between local communities may be traced in the records of businesses such Odlums whose connections extended across a range of localities including Dublin, Sallins, Tullamore and other midland towns. The Odlums archives in the NAI include minute books and account books, ledgers and day books, which record specific transactions between the company and the neighbouring community. The accounting records in the NAI and PRONI are wide ranging and include cost books, ledgers and day books as well as quotations books, valuation records and other operational records – all of which provide researchers with representations of the company or organization's perspective on local business practice in Ireland.

Credit ratings and the systematization of local knowledge

Jeacle and Walsh, whose work forms the first brief case study in this chapter, characterize the development of formal credit rating systems as a means of 'systematizing local knowledge'.[24] The use by banks of directories (for example, Wilson's *Dublin Directory with additions*. 1789–) as a means of developing and recording credit rating information has already been noted. Although credit ratings were ostensibly based on economic criteria, assessment of 'moral character' was also an important factor in constructing a profile of the customer (or potential customer).[25]

In her original work on women in Ireland between 1500 and 1800, Mary O'Dowd has made excellent use of Wilson's *Dublin Directory* to assess the financial and economic activity of women in a systematic way, monitoring the length of

22 Keith Hoskin and Richard Macve, 'The genesis of accountability: the West Point connections' in *Accounting, Organizations and Society*, 13 (1988), pp 37–73; Loft, 'Towards a critical understanding of accounting', pp 137–71; Jeacle & Walsh, 'From moral evaluation to rationalization', pp 737–61.   23 Professor Purcell was appointed peat investigation officer to the Fuel Research Department in 1918 and was instrumental in introducing the milling of peat for briquettes: see C.S. Andrews, 'Some precursors of Bord Na Mona', paper read before the Statistical and Social Inquiry Society of Ireland on 30 Apr. 1954, reproduced in *Journal of the Statistical and Social Inquiry Society of Ireland*, 19:2 (1953/54), pp 132–55.   24 Jeacle & Walsh, 'From moral evaluation to rationalization', p. 742.   25 Richard Leigh, *Elements of retailing* (New York, 1923).

time they were in business.[26] From O'Dowd's work it is possible to get a sense of the various ways in which businesses engaged with individuals, including vulnerable members of the community such as widows. Furthermore, as O'Dowd notes, private correspondence can be a valuable source of information on women's involvement in family estates and households. She alerts historians' attention to the fact that during the seventeenth century 'women like the 1st duchess of Ormond wrote more private letters, usually in their own hand, but they were still largely impersonal and businesslike in tone and usually concerned with estate management and family accounts'.[27] On a related note, family papers such as those of the house of Ormond,[28] which primarily cover Kilkenny and Tipperary, illuminate aspects of the business history of the relevant counties as they typically contain documents related to land grants and matters of credit. For example, in a letter to Lord Ormond dated 20 June 1660, the author, Francis Tuke, states that 'the lands of Carrokehoe and Garrenconnell, in the county of Kilkenny, – containing about 700 acres, – were put upon me, towards satisfaction of my arrears'.[29]

For the historian grappling to ascertain the creditworthiness of a specific individual or to track the payment patterns of members of a local community, debtors records held in accounts will prove especially informative. These are transaction-based records. Hence, the account books of businesses involved in retail credit (for example, the Lucan Estate, MAYO 13; John McGing, MAYO 14 and Messrs Carey Walsh Ltd, MAYO 25) is particularly informative for monitoring payment patterns and bad debts in a local community over a prolonged period.

Politics and business

Andy Bielenberg's work on the distillery industry in Kilbeggan effectively highlights the way in which a significant local industry, Locke's Distillery, responded to local and national developments, the former largely economic, the latter political.[30] Politics had always impinged on local businesses, as Cullen makes clear in relation to the eighteenth century, citing examples of canal construction and insurance companies. He goes on to emphasize the connection between politics and business, explaining that the 'background to canal companies and insurance companies reflected for the first time the presence of mixed politician and business groups:

26 Mary O'Dowd, *A history of women in Ireland, 1500–1800* (Harlow, 2005), pp 120–4. **27** Ibid., p. 227. **28** The electronic calendar of the Carte papers, 1660–87, Bodleian Library, University of Oxford: 'the Ormond papers among the Carte MSS are the major source for the Civil War and Restoration era in Irish history. In effect, they form the archive of the royal administration there, but their significance goes far beyond this. Many of the original records of the Irish administration were destroyed as a result of war and fires from the 18th to the 20th centuries' (http://www.bodley.ox.ac.uk/dept/scwmss/projects/carte/carte.html) **29** http://www.bodley.ox.ac.uk/dept/scwmss/projects/carte/carte30.html, MS Carte 30, fol. 701. **30** Andy Bielenberg, *Locke's Distillery: a history* (Dublin, 1993).

inevitably, given the competitive or divided nature of Irish political society, these activities tended to be duplicated: two politically different ways were projected even for reaching by canal from Dublin the river Shannon in the Irish midlands.'[31]

Church records

A largely untapped corpus of business records lies in the archives of various Church organizations. Like landlords, Churches were significant economic agencies operating at local level the length and breadth of the country and, of course, prior to Dis-Establishment (1869) the Church of Ireland in particular was a significant landowner. Furthermore, many Catholic religious orders left extensive collections of archival material which are potentially rich sources for the business historian. As part of the Women's History Project that examined over 300 repositories, Maria Luddy found that many convent archives include account books. Given that by 1900 most towns as well as cities in Ireland had at least one convent, these archives represent very important sources of information about the orders' dealings with various businesses. For example, the archives of the Dominican Convent at Channel Row in Dublin contain accounts and receipts books dating from 1719.[32] This material is available for consultation at the Dominican Archives in Cabra, Dublin.[33] Among these accounts are records of payment of 10s. 10d. for 'opening Mrs Bellew's grave' and 17s. 4d. for 'cakes and wine for ye clergy'.[34] Various religious orders ran large institutions such as hospitals and in such cases usually the central archives of the order holds material relating to their business methods. Luddy has clearly shown the extensive range of business enterprises associated with convents in the nineteenth century.[35] In addition to operating as quasi-businesses, the involvement of certain religious orders in the management of various medical institutions also compelled them to conduct transactions with the members of the local communities which they served. From large Dublin hospitals to impoverished poorhouses in local communities across Ireland, these surviving records contain a wealth of insights into many aspects of local businesses.[36] Further afield, Irish religious also impacted on business developments and effectively capitalized on Irish contacts in their locales as they deemed appropriate.[37]

31 L.M. Cullen, 'The evolution of mercantile cultures and values in western Europe in the seventeenth and eighteenth centuries: the changing status of merchants' in *Fiere e mercanti nella integrazione delle economie europee (sece. XIII–XVIII)*, 32 (2001), pp 1001–38: p. 1032. Our thanks to Professor Cullen for giving us a copy of his article.   **32** Maria Luddy, 'Convent archives as sources for Irish history' in Rosemary Raughter (ed.), *Religious women and their history. Breaking the silence* (Dublin, 2005), pp 98–115: p. 114.   **33** Thanks to Sr Terence O'Keefe for all her help with the Dominican Archives in Cabra. For work on Dominican education in Ireland, see Máire M. Kealy, *Dominican education in Ireland, 1820–1930* (Dublin, 2007).   **34** Quoted in Leon Ó Broin, *Miss Crookshank agus coirp eile* (Dublin, 1951), p. 63.   **35** Maria Luddy, *Women and philanthropy in nineteenth-century Ireland* (Cambridge, 1995), p. 52.   **36** Brian Donnelly and Margaret Ó hÓgartaigh, 'Medical archives for the socio-economic historian' in *Irish Economic & Social History*, 27 (2000), pp 66–72.   **37** For Irish,

Some locally generated sources

Tom O'Neill has pointed out that in the printing industry, from the nineteenth century, the 'backbone of the business was a newspaper'. He also advises researchers that of 'all the business archives, those of the law firms would be expected to be the richest in the historical material which they contain.' Business firms are certainly well represented in solicitors' files.[38] Another previously mentioned untapped source for business history are the often voluminous estate records. For example, the archives of the Emo estate in County Laois contain extensive records of business transactions between the earl of Portarlington and his many clients. Among these, the earl's farming journal gives a unique insight into the commercial aspects of agriculture in Ireland during the first half of the nineteenth century.[39]

Furthermore, locally generated literature is also a potentially significant resource. Patricia J. Anderson and Jonathan Rose's edited volume on literary publishing houses includes essays on Browne & Nolan of Dublin, McGlashan & Gill of Dublin (later M.H. Gill & Son and Gill & MacMillan) and Simms & McIntyre of Belfast as well as a study of the Cuala Press. Similarly, Robert Hogan's *Dictionary of Irish literature* features a number of entries on Irish publishers and their archives. Focusing on magazines produced at local level in both the Republic of Ireland and Northern Ireland, Tom Clyde has published a very useful guide to a plethora of titles in which he provides details of their place of publication, editors and issue dates. Such sources offer potentially useful insights to local historians on local publishing business and, more generally, into those publications' place in local life.[40]

For the late medieval and early modern periods valuable work by Jane Ohlmeyer and Éamonn Ó Ciardha on the Irish staple[41] gives an insight into busi-

---

female, ecclesiastical entrepreneurs in England and Wales, see Barbara Walsh, *Roman Catholic nuns in England and Wales, 1800–1937* (Dublin, 2002), pp 89–124; for the USA see Barbra Mann Wall, *Unlikely entrepreneurs. Catholic sisters and the hospital marketplace, 1865–1925* (Columbus, OH, 2005). **38** Tom O'Neill, 'Newspapers and journals', p. 1 and idem, 'Estate, family and business records', pp 14–5 (unpublished lectures) in Tom O'Neill papers, NLI, Acc. 5040, Box 3. **39** This journal has been published privately and is available at Emo House in County Laois: see John S. Powell (ed.), *'Shot a buck ...', the Emo estate, 1798–1852. Documents of Portarlington, no. 3* (Portarlington, n.d.); see also Dooley, *Sources for the history of landed estates in Ireland* (Dublin, 2000). **40** Patricia J. Anderson and Jonathan Rose (eds), *Dictionary of literary biography: volume 106, British literary publishing houses, 1820–1880* (London, 1991); idem (eds), *Dictionary of literary biography: volume 112, British literary publishing houses, 1881–1965* (London, 1991); Robert Hogan, *Dictionary of Irish literature* (London, 1996); Tom Clyde, *Irish literary magazines: an outline history and descriptive biography* (Dublin, 2003). We are grateful to Joanne Wydenbach for alerting us to this material. **41** 'The Staple of England, Ireland and Wales was established in the late 13th century by Edward I. Under ordinances which were promulgated by that monarch in 1291, wool, leather and sheepskins were designated as the *staple*, or basis, items of merchandise and these could be sold to foreign merchants only in named towns, which became known as *staple towns*. Dublin was on

ness activities in Dublin, Cork and Drogheda for a comparatively poorly documented era. The Irish staple was initially established 'to regulate the trade of basic,
or staple, goods which could only be sold to foreign merchants in designated
'staple' towns and provided a sure way for traders to recover their debts. By the
early seventeenth century the real significance of the staple lay in the regulation of
debt and the creation of a sophisticated credit network.' The CDROM of the
staple book, which includes lists of creditors and debtors and the database contains
all transactions, is of particular value to local historians focussing on these ports.[42]

Traces of cosmopolitanism and globalization in the Irish locale

In addition to the published narratives and travelogues of visitors to Ireland which
became increasingly numerous from the eighteenth century onwards, local historians can glean evidence of individuals passing through cities and town throughout
Ireland in business archives. As noted in Appendix 1, hotel files occasionally contain visitors' books: the book for Glynn's hotel in Gort, County Galway can be
consulted in the NAI (GAL 8/1). Each entry states who the guest(s) was/were and
where they came from (see, for example, entry for '2/8/1947: Reginald Nolan and
wife from London'). In some cases, visitors also noted their previous and future
destinations. These records can be used by the historian to gauge how busy the
hotel was, especially on special occasions coinciding with a particular event in the
city or town. They may also be analyzed with a view to constructing a profile of
visitors to the hotel and indeed to the area more generally; for example, on 30 July
1947 there were four visitors staying in Glynn's hotel who came from Ireland,
England and the US, indicating a degree of 1940s cosmopolitanism (albeit not of
the continental European variety). Similar records are held in the NAI for Leen's
hotel in Abbeyfeale, County Limerick (LIM 16) and for Mrs Leen's Temperance
hotel in Westport, County Mayo (MAYO 16).[43] Leslie Clarkson's aforementioned
work on hospitality, housekeeping and high living in eighteenth-century Ireland
unveils patterns of hospitality in another local context, namely the Big House. In
the process, he casts fascinating light on the comings and goings of visitors and their
consumption in localities throughout the country. The sources used by Clarkson
to construct this analysis are outlined in chapter two and represent only a sample of
the wide ranging archival material that is at the disposal of local historians undertaking similar studies of hospitality and consumption patterns for Big Houses across
the country.

three staple towns nominated under the 1291 ordinances, the other two being Drogheda
and Cork.' See Mary Clark, *The archives of the Dublin staple, 1596–1678* (Dublin, 1996). **42**
Jane Ohlmeyer, 'Calculating debt: the Irish statue staple records' in *Irish Economic & Social
History*, 27 (2000), pp 63–5: p. 65; idem, 'The statute staple in early modern Ireland: com-
piling a historical database' in *History Ireland*, 6:4 (Winter 1998), pp 36–40; idem and
Éamonn Ó Ciardha (eds), *The Irish statute staple books, 1596–1687* (Dublin, 1998).   **43**
Temperance hotels were to be found in various locations throughout Ireland and (pre-
dictably) were noted for not serving alcohol.

CASE STUDIES

Case study 1: 'The role of local knowledge'

Published studies: I. Jeacle and E. Walsh, 'The taming of the buyer: the retail inventory method and the early twentieth-century department store' in *Accounting, Organizations and Society*, 28 (2003), pp 773–91 and idem, 'From moral evaluation to rationalization: accounting and the shifting technologies of credit' in *Accounting Organizations and Society*, 27 (2002), pp 737–61.

Archival sources used: Credit rating archives of McBirney's department store (NAI, G1/i).

Rationale and methodology: Arguing (p. 739) that 'the advent of mass credit facilities during the early decades of the twentieth century prompted department stores to abandon traditional cash only trading', Ingrid Jeacle and Eamonn Walsh have drawn upon the credit rating archives of McBirney's department store (NAI, G1/i). The authors begin (p. 739) by identifying 'the role of local knowledge in the maintenance of a credit nexus' asserting that 'The nature of this local knowledge was such that it was embodied in individuals rather than institutions'. Based on her doctoral study, Jeacle used *inter alia* two ledgers detailing the credit risk of every account customer in the period 1920s–30s in order to construct a profile of that store's customers and to conceptualize the 'shifting technologies of credit' in the early twentieth century. The ledgers – in alphabetical order – contain the list of customers, the date on which credit facilities were sought and a record of the personal circumstances of each credit applicant. As such, these are important sources of information on the business's perception of individuals which is often based on hearsay, gossip and observation. Some of the commentaries which formed the basis of clients' credit ratings are reproduced in the aforementioned 2002 paper (see also Table 5).

Table 5: Credit rating material in the McBirney's archive

---

1. Examples of the extent of detailed personal information on customers

22/10/1923   Bookkeeper in X Flour Mills for past year. Yearly tenant of furnished private house. Value of furniture about £100. Salary about £4 per week. Prompt in payments and safe for amount £25. Steady. Sober. Married no children.

24/1/1925   Has been building cottages for Rathdrum District Council for past 3 years, and is at present building 3 cottages for Shillelagh DC. Also carries on T. Quarries, and seems to be doing very well, as he employs a good many men.

12/2/1925   Was governess to Mrs K for her 2 sons, now at school in Dublin. Miss G is staying with Mrs K over 15 years and is now acting as lady's companion; drives Mrs Ks motor car, and assists in her house. She is most respectable, and I think she has private means.

10/10/1925   X, ex-Lieut. F.S. Army is principal partner. It is said there is a foreigner behind it. Cannot ascertain owing to his short time in business, whether he would be sale but he is said to have had a considerable sum when leaving the Army.

22/10/1928   Carries on business as a dairy farmer and pays someone to look after the business. He is a teacher at the school mentioned and is very respectable and financially sound. Considered sale for your figures.

8/11/1928   Wife of X a small farmer carrying on a dairy business, sending milk to Dublin by train and very industrious. Mrs X has not a good name for payments but with her husband's sanction credit named is quite in order.

18/6/1929   Several years at address which he rents and is employed as a salesman by X Ltd. He is said to be highly respectable and nothing is known against him, though his financial position is not regarded as too strong. He is [*sic.*] been ill for some time past but is now all right again. Mrs B is said to be living beyond her means and in view of this informants hesitate to advise £50 credit. but consider up to £20 a fair trade risk.

25/1/1930   I am reliably informed that she recently was inmate of a private mental hospital. Would strongly advise obtaining her father's approval.

28/8/1930   Wife of Mr A, at one time connected with the X Co. Very respectable, steady man, said to own his own house, but not regarded as too strong financially. However, he is very well regarded locally, always pays his way and nothing is known against him.

2. Examples of the importance of personal knowledge of customers

23/10/1924   Mrs F (wife of Linens buyer) a native of Drogheda stated this was a very good family living in best part of the town and should be quite all right.

1/2/1928   A sister of Mr C. Good as gold.

14/10/1929   Known to Mr F who says she is an old cash customer.

19/3/1930   Brother of X who says he is a professor of music in Y school. This was confirmed by Mr A who says he is a very respectable man. Mr X states he owns this house and has a motor car.

18/5/1930   Mr C (silks dept) says: Next door neighbours of mine. Own the house and are OK.

3. Examples of the importance of property and/or position in granting credit

15/2/1924   At address for 15 years. Has all exterior appearances of well to do person and has no other business than keeping first class lodgers. Safe for credit named.

7/6/1924   Married woman. Husband living. Own a large property in America. Quite sale for credit named.

22/7/1929   Wife of a police pensioner who is also a clerk and rent agent. They have a nice private house and are in comfortable circumstances. I consider credit named alright.

17/10/1929   First class people, have a beautiful place and should be all right.

11/2/1930   Employed as accountant in Rathmines. a permanent and pensionable post. Runs two motor cars. Respectable and nothing is known against him.

12/6/1930   These people are gentlemen farmers in a very big way and are quite all right.

18/6/1930   Wife of Dr. B, dispensary Dr. Resides with her husband and family in a private residence with 17 acres of land attached. Respectable and said to be well off.

31/6/1930   Wife of Mr. X, an ex-officer of the R.I.C. who retired with county inspector's rank. Has about £500 p.a. pension and is regarded as a very solvent man and should prove safe for the credit named.

Source: Jeacle & Walsh, 'From moral evaluation to rationalization: accounting and the shifting technologies of credit', drawn from NAI, G1/i. The names of the customers are excluded for reasons of confidentiality.

Jeacle and Walsh's use of these credit rating archival sources is an interesting example of how accounting technologies can shed light, in a macro-sense, on broader trends in society and, in a micro-sense, on individuals in that society. Further, as Jeacle and Walsh argue, in an age of expanding credit, local knowledge formed the basis on which credit decisions were based and that knowledge in turn was 'systematised' through the reporting mechanisms adopted by McBirney's. Their work provides a model for similar studies. Analysis of retail records for other businesses throughout the country may uncover similar or dissimilar stories in various local contexts (see Table 6 for details of other retail archives in the NAI and PRONI which contain potentially useful data to support such studies).

Table 6: Grocers and merchant records in the NAI

DUB 89	McBirney and Co. Ltd	department store		1830–1983	minute books, account books, correspondence, invoices, deeds and leases
DUB 139	Pim Brothers	department store		20th Century	account correspondence
KK 4	Nolan	general merchant	Goresbridge	1873–1915	
KER 10	J.M. Reidy	general merchant	Killarney	1897–1962	
WEX 16		general merchant, bar and post office	Kilmuckridge	1831–1909	
DUB 87	Hortons	gents outfitters		1925–85	accounts, miscelllaneous material
CL 5	Murphy	grocer	Mullagh	1943–46	account book
SLIGO 16	Martin Timmoney	grocer	Cliffoney	1902–72	day books, customers ledgers, invoices
KK 1	Mulhall	grocer and baker	Kilkenny	1889–1959	
LOU 24	J. Berrill	grocer and egg merchant	Drogheda	1897–	cash books, stock books, letter books, egg account books
TIPP 14	Hamill	grocer and publican	Cloughjordan	1916–73	accounts
KK 5	Patrick Grace	grocer and publican	Ballyragget	1912–73	counter books, day books, ledgers
CAR 18	E.J. Doyle	grocer and vintner	Ballon	1877–1901	bills and receipts
KK 12	Bowden	grocer, bar, hardware	Urlingford	1869–1939	
LOU 1	Carroll	grocer, bar, undertaker	Dunleer	1865–1911	account books
CAR 6	Coady	grocer, draper, corn and wool merchant	Borris	1863–1948	
OFF 7	Scully	grocer, grain merchant	Kilcormac	1890–1964	
DUB 124	Leverett and Frye	grocers and wine merchants	Ranelagh	1912–27	wages book

MAYO 25	Messrs Carey Walsh Ltd	grocers, drapers, sawmillers and hardware merchants	Newport	1909–49	account books and correspondence
MAYO 24	M. Mulloy & Sons	grocers, ironmongers and importers	Westport	1859–	account books, letter books
DUB 123	Robert Smyth & Sons Ltd	grocers, wine and cigar merchants		1822–3	day books
MAYO 5		grocery	Westport	1883–1923	day books
WICK 29		grocery	Wicklow	1861–3	account book
CAR 4	Dalton	grocery and bar	Borris	1869–1922	
MAYO 14	John McGing	grocery and bar	Westport	1874–1935	sales and purchases books

Source: Drawn from Ó hÓgartaigh & Ó hÓgartaigh, Database of Corporate Governance Archives, http://www.ucd.ie/research/people/business/databaseacga/

Case study 2: Locating international research in local history

Published study: R. Craig, C. Ó hÓgartaigh and M. Ó hÓgartaigh, 'Clowns of no account? Reflections on the involvement of four Irishmen in the commercial life of the New South Wales colony, 1788–1818' in *Accounting History*, 9, no. 2 (2004), pp 63–86.

Archival sources used: Business textbooks (NLI); *Fourth Report of the Commissioners of the Irish Education Inquiry, 1826–1827 (London: 1826–1827)* (NLI)

Rationale and methodology: This article grew out of a previous study which involved an exploration of the educational background of a number of Irishmen who went to the New South Wales colony between 1792 and 1805. One of these, John Kenny from County Carlow, placed an advertisement in the *Sydney Gazette* on 4 October 1806 as a teacher of accounting. It would appear that Kenny was educated in one of Carlow's hedge-schools and contemporary sources suggest that book-keeping was part of the curriculum taught in some hedge schools in late eighteenth- and early nineteenth-century Ireland. Furthermore, the *Report of the Commissioners of Irish Education Enquiry* indicated that there were several hedge schools in the Carlow area. This article provides a useful example of combining evidence from a variety of business (business textbooks) and non-business (*Report of the Commissioners on Irish Education Enquiry*) sources in order to gain an understanding of the local environment which Irish emigrants left behind. Secondly, it shows how historians can extend that understanding from the local to an international context. Evidence recorded in business textbooks indicated the existence of an accounting education being available in Ireland's 'hedge schools' while the *Report of the Commissioners on Irish Education Enquiry* provided concrete, verifiable evidence of the existence of such schools in specific localities. Drawing on this research and on the work of Bill Reece[44] and Patrick O'Farrell,[45] Craig et al. con-

44 Bob Reece, 'Irish convicts and Australian historians' in idem (ed.), *Irish convicts: the origins of convicts transported to Australia* (Dublin, 1989).   45 Patrick O'Farrell, *The Irish in*

cluded (p. 78) that this local evidence suggested that a figure such as John Kenny 'represented the "sameness and circularity" (Said, 1993, p. 127) which confirmed old power in a new world'. With migration, the characteristics of an education acquired in a specific local context extended beyond the orbit of the local to an international context and audience. As this study demonstrates, the implications of researching a local institution, such as a school, are not therefore limited to the local – important though this may be – but can also shed light on historical experiences of émigrés at national and international levels.

This chapter has sought to detail the potential uses of major records within business archives by local historians. While the archive is clearly a very important source of evidence, it should be regarded as the means rather than the end of understanding and findings gleaned from the contents of that archive need to be placed and interpreted in their temporal and geographical context. Business archives are particularly enlightening windows on the world of past communities throughout Ireland and their engagement with the wider world. The conclusion discusses the contextual analysis of business archives further, putting business in its place.

Australia (2nd ed., Sydney, 2000).

Conclusion: putting business in its place

The archival material identified in this guide presents both opportunities and challenges to the local historian. The opportunities lie in the potential for business archives (through their detailed record of transactions and events) to illuminate multiple aspects of the life of a local community. Business was and still is a focus of local activity, a fulcrum around which local community life often revolves. Businesses, in that context, are frequently an important – if sometimes overlooked – element of a local community's life. Increasingly, business and accounting historians see their archival sources not only as a lens through which one can observe the minutiae of business life but also a rich seam of evidence pointing to the reality that business shaped the very *milieu* of a local community's life. As has been emphasized in this guide, all business was transacted within a specific temporal, social, economic and geographic context: consequently, historians can reach a deeper understanding of that context through imaginative analysis of business records.

Further, apart from being an important part of local life, to varying degrees businesses have served historians well as valuable record-keepers of ordinary and extraordinary aspects of life in their particular time and place. Their records generally served two purposes, private and/or public. The private records – encompassing, for example, journal and ledger entries, credit assessments and other internal accounts – represent an internal dialogue within the business entity, a record kept to assist management in making decisions. Such records may vary in detail and format but they are none the less illustrative of the engagement of commerce with its locale and, through that lens, they constitute representations of the locale itself. The public record – including, for example, minute books, advertisements and (mainly in the case of larger organizations) annual accounts – serves a different, wider, often regulatory or legal purpose. Given the regulatory context, such records are more likely to follow a prescribed pattern, laid down by legislation or traditional practice. Moreover, the dialogue in this case is between the business and its public. This has a number of implications for the local historian. Businesses engage with several stakeholders who, separately and together, constitute their local community: investors, employees (who are by their nature local), suppliers, customers, competitors, the public at large and, in particular in this case, neighbours. The information recorded and reproduced in such instances sheds light not only on the business itself but also on its relationship with the local community in all its guises. Such public information may be especially significant in explaining a business's decline[1] and/or success as well as the cycle of corporate and local life and, in that

---

[1] This may be particularly the case given that the information in archives are often deposited by companies which are no longer in business (see, for example, Sugar Company records from Carlow and Thurles (NAI, CAR 2006/38)).

setting, its engagement with and influence on the socio-economic history of a local area. In the case of publicly disclosed information, the business archive may project a perspective which it wants – or needs – to portray. Legal and other requirements may prompt the business to disclose what it otherwise would not. Further, records often reflect the business's own view of its position in that world. It may seek legitimacy, approval, investment or other forms of validation: it may, on the other hand, seek anonymity and wish to avoid scrutiny. In such cases, the business is attempting to construct an image of itself in the minds of the local population and the processes of construction that underpin such information are an important element in our understanding of the corporate persona and its engagement with the world. Often, what is not said or how what is said is framed is illuminating in such contexts.[2]

This construction of the business archive brings us to comment on some of the main challenges this material presents for the local historian. Local historians should note that these accounting, business and corporate records often contain representations of reality as much as – or more than – reality itself. Business records offer a vista on the past through a limited, hand-crafted lens. The perspective is limited in scope as business will often – though not always – observe the world for business reasons and with business tools of recognition and measurement. Hence, not all events – even business events – may be recognized or recorded in the business archive: only those of interest from a particular perspective at a particular time. Those that are documented may be recorded for a specific purpose or in a way that is difficult for the researcher to understand. Furthermore, as with any archive, business records are the product of their authors. This can be especially problematic in business as there may be monetary or regulatory outcomes at stake which motivate the disclosure in a certain direction. This may give rise to non-disclosure and/or selective, self-interested or biased disclosure which ultimately gives rise to an archive that portrays a very particular, contrived view of the world. Hence, working with the material preserved in the business archive demands a high level of care on the researcher's part. The sources should be sifted and compared with other sources in an effort to gain as balanced, rounded and informed a view of the local, historical world in which they were generated as possible. Often, internal and external sources of business information can be compared for consistency and inconsistency by using a number of sources, each providing a different perspective on events. The role of the historian is to judge the evidence presented in an effort to reflect the 'truth' as accurately as possible. This is no less the case with business records: while the quantitative, quasi-official nature of such records may be enveloped in an aura of reliability, they are not immune from the limitations of any historical source.[3]

2 Ruth D. Hines and Shane R. Moriarity, 'Understanding accounting in its social and historical context' in *Accounting Review*, 65:1 (1990), pp 286–7; Ruth D. Hines, 'Financial accounting: in communicating reality, we construct reality' in *Accounting, Organizations and Society*, 13:3 (1988), pp 251–61. **3** G.R. Elton, *Return to essentials. Some reflections on the current state of historical study* (Cambridge, 1991); Richard Evans, *In defence of history* (London,

Conscious of such caveats, local historians, through the special perspectives that they can bring to bear on historical research, have the potential to add greatly to our understanding of business history. The value of the business archive is two-fold. The construction of context – in particular local context – in business history can illuminate the conflicts and compromises associated with business as well as, potentially, highlighting the motivations behind the actions of businesses and business people. Businesses are shaped and incentivized by their engagement with their stakeholders. These stakeholders are often members of the local community in which they exist and through which they have economic and social meaning. As a consequence, the task of the local historian in putting business in its place and in knitting together the threads of corporation and community is a very important one in a commercial world increasingly focused on the global and the globalized.

[handwritten annotations]

① Development of Accounting Paradigms?

② Value Added Accounting

③ As Well – Push Budget Sources

1997); Marriner, 'Company financial statements as source material for business historians'; Lee, 'The changing form of the Corporate Annual Report'; Ó hÓgartaigh et al., '"How it essentially was"'.

Catalogue number	Name	Industry sector	Local area	Period	Other notes
**	Dublin Port & Docks Board	port	Dublin	1708–1945	
**	Swiftbrook Paper Mills, Saggart (Clondalkin Paper Mills)	papermills	Dublin	1831–1925	
**	Guinness & Mahon	merchant bankers and land agents	Dublin	1837–1962	
**	Stock Exchange	stock exchange	Dublin	1802–1978	
**	Alliance & Consumers Gas Co.	gas distribution	Dublin	from 1830s	
**	Battersby's	estate agents	Dublin	1855–1973	
**	Arnott & Co.	department store	Dublin	1871–	account books, minute books
**	Switzer & Co.	department store	Dublin	1890–	account books, minute books
1028	Sick and Indigent Roomkeepers' Society	charity	Dublin	20th century	administrative and operational records
1072	Jacob's	biscuit manufacturers	Dublin	1888–1964	wages
1091	Irish Industrial Development Association	industry development		1906–97	
1120	Royal Irish Academy of Music	music		1856–1955	
1150	Ceimici Teoranta	chemicals		1935–86	audited accounts, correspondence files, operational files

Catalogue number	Name	Industry sector	Local area	Period	Other notes
2001/95	Eircom (formerly Telecom Eireann)	communications company		1870–	administrative and operational records, maps, plans and drawings relating to telecommunication in Ireland from the take-over of the telegraph network to the present day
97/40	St John's Hospital	hospital	Sligo	20th century	operational records
97/48	Graves & Co.	shipowners and timber merchants	New Ross	1844–69	correspondence
98/40	United Stationary Engine Drivers, Boilermen, Cranemen, Motormen's and Machinemen's Trade Union	trade union	Limerick	1914–72	minute book, income and expenditure books, subscriptions and levies books
Acc. No. 1007	Irish Distillers Ltd	distilling			Powers from 1870; Jamesons from 1819
BG 79	Dublin Union	poor house	Dublin	20th century	
CAR 1	Traynor	auctioneer and insurance agent	Carlow	1841–1936	general ledger
CAR 2	Young	auctioneer, estate and insurance agent	Muine Bheag	1888–1937	
CAR 4	Dalton	grocery and bar	Borris	1869–1922	
CAR 6	Coady	grocer, draper, corn and wool merchant	Borris	1863–1948	
CAR 14	John Rice	sack supplier	Carlow	1946–61	sack hire books
CAR 15	Thomas Thompson & Son Ltd, Hanover Works	structural engineers and manufacturers	Carlow	1826–1970	account books, wages books, damp press letter books, correspondence,

Reference	Name	Business	Place	Dates	Records
		of specialized machinery			catalogues including records of the Nepture Iron Works, Waterford, 1856–78; the Irish Boring Company (1940) Ltd, 1940–54; the Waterford (Bilberry) Brick Company, 1920–47
CAR 17	William A. Young	veterinary surgeon	Tullow	1887–91	account books
CAR 18	E.J. Doyle	grocer and vintner	Ballon	1901–04	bills and receipts
CAR 19	Carlow Gas Co.	gas company	Carlow	1877–1901	minute books
CAR 20	John J. Duggan	solicitor	Carlow	1847–1933	legal papers
CARLOW 2006/38	Irish Sugar Co.	sugar processing	Carlow, Tuam and Thurles	19th century; 1926–	administrative and operational records, 500 boxes
CL 2	Roche Kelly	oil mills	Sixmilebridge	1762–1897	
CL 3	McMahon	estate and insurance agents	Ennis	1666–1966	
CL 4	Glynn	flour and meal mills	Kilrush	1884–1966	account book
CL 5	Murphy	grocer	Mullagh	1943–6	income and expenditure books, lace
CL 7	Presentation Convent	convent	Youghal	1832–1945	account books
COR 2	William Stockdale	merchant	Cork	1759–77	account book and general note book
CORK 2005/166	National Bank Ltd	bank	Cork	1920	memorandum regarding procedures to be carried out in the event of outrages against bank property carried out by auxiliaries and soldiers
CORK 2006/104	Bank of Ireland	bank	Cork	1927, 1935–6	securities books
DON 3	Henry Kee	auctioneer	Stranorlar	1880–1902	letting book
DON 14	Hammond & Sweeney	auctioneers and undertakers	Donegal	1914–20; 1930–36	ledgers

Catalogue number	Name	Industry sector	Local area	Period	Other notes
DON 21	Stewart Estates	land/estate	Donegal	1818–1941	rentals and rent ledgers
DON 24	Thomas Swan	flour mills	Buncrana	1920–60	(includes some of the records of the Buncrana Electric Co.)
DON 26	John Wray and Co.	solicitors	Rathmelton	1892–1942	business accounts
DON 27	Convoy Woollen Mills	woollen mills	Convoy	1803–1987	audited accounts, account books, reports, files, minute books, wages
DUB 5	Lisney & Co.	auctioneers	Dublin	1852–1959	
DUB 6	Kildare Street Club	men's club	Dublin	1905–70	
DUB 10	North Dublin Milling Co.	flour mills	Dublin	1874–1978	
DUB 12	Standard Life Assurance	insurance	Dublin	1847–96	also Sun Life Assurance, 1814–
DUB 21	Mercer's Hospital	hospital	Dublin	1750–1945	
DUB 22	Rotunda Hospital	hospital	Dublin	1797–	
DUB 26	Cummins	sanitary engineers		1877–1948	
DUB 28	Ferrier Pollock & Co.	warehousing	Dublin	1803–14	bills and bonds
DUB 29	Kiernan	brush manufacturers		1887–1970	
DUB 29	W.C. McCormick	coal merchant and ship broker		1852–1900	account books
DUB 41	Robert Smyth & Co. of the Green	merchant, retailer	Dublin	1738–1966	
DUB 43	Balls Bank	banking		c.1797–c.1897	
DUB 44	John C. Parkes & Sons Ltd	electricians, die sinkers and iron steel and tin-plate merchants	Dublin	1844–86	account book
DUB 47	John Ireland & Son Ltd	uniform clothing manufacturers	Dublin	1940–67	accounts
DUB 48	J.M. Daly	chemist	Dublin	1959–63	prescription book

DUB 49	I. Lightfoot & Sons Ltd	fruit and vegetable salesmen	Dublin	1945–9	workmen's account book
DUB 50	Valentine Morgan	victualler	Dublin	1908–21	day book
DUB 51	Kevin Rafferty	publican	Dublin	1929–35	day book
DUB 52	Inchicore Model Schools	school	Dublin	1849–1920	roll book, inspector's book, accounts
DUB 53	Wilcox Jozeau (Ireland) Ltd	wholesale chemists	Dublin	1929–38	nominal ledger
DUB 54	Mater Misericordiae Hospital	hospital	Dublin	1887–1949	operations register
DUB 55	Coombe Hospital	hospital	Dublin	1864–1972	audited accounts, annual reports, minute books, reports and accounts, charter, deeds, leases some from 1890
DUB 56	Dublin Laundry Co.	laundry		1888–1982	wages books, invoices, incoming and outgoing correspondence, operations and account books, family papers (1812–1904), minute books, private ledgers, abstracts of accounts, photographs, 1888–1970
DUB 57	Dublin Workingmen's Club	workingmen's club	Dublin	1897–1965	minutes, registers of members and account books
DUB 58	Cantwell's	wine merchants	Dublin	1875–1970	account books, correspondence
DUB 59	B. O'Connell	footwear repairer	Dublin	1948–9	day book
DUB 60	Roche's	chemists	Dublin	1931–60	prescription books
DUB 61	Peter Breen	motor engineer	Dublin	1905–75	day books, car sales book, abstracts of accounts
DUB 62	James Hunt	tobacco and cigar manufacturer and retailer	Dublin	1833–69	house sales book, day books, ledgers

Catalogue number	Name	Industry sector	Local area	Period	Other notes
DUB 63	Dublin Tuberculosis Hospitals	hospital	Dublin	1942–65	admission and discharge registers, treatments register, press cuttings book
DUB 64	Irish Mining Co.	mining	Dublin	1885–1969	cash books, ledgers, sales and purchases books, wages books
DUB 65	Gordon's Hardware	hardware	Dublin	1963–71	ledger
DUB 66	Johnston's Pharmacy	pharmacy	Dublin	1924–7	personal ledger
DUB 67	Victor Fitzpatrick	motor engineer	Dublin	1948–62	account books and sales books
DUB 68	Kelly Brothers	victuallers	Dublin	1943–69	account books
DUB 69	Boland's Mills	mills	Dublin	1880–1982	minute books, agenda books, operations books, stock and share material, correspondence files, deeds and leases, plans and drawings
DUB 70	Micheal MacNamara & Sons	leaf tobacco importers	Dublin	1832–59; 1898–1945	ledgers
DUB 71	Mitchell's	outfitters	Dublin	1916–29	ledgers
DUB 72	Dublin Evening Mail	newspaper	Dublin	1896, 1926–55	day books
DUB 73	The French Wreath Shop	retail	Dublin	1952–66	ledgers
DUB 74	L.J. McNally	watchmakers and jewellers	Dublin	1942–5	job books
				1903–53	rent books and papers
DUB 75	Donnelly (Dublin) Ltd	bacon factors	Dublin	1880–1980	minute books, account books, deeds and leases
DUB 77	Dublin Stock Exchange	stock exchange	Dublin	1802–1961	registers and daily lists
DUB 78	Bryson's	tailors	Dublin	1967–9	order book
DUB 79	Fannin & Co.	surgical instruments	Dublin	1867–1971	minute books, accounts, audited accounts and private ledgers, 1895–1973
DUB 81	Winstanley Ltd	shoemakers	Dublin	1930–80	accounts, operational books, files
DUB 83	John H. Drought Ltd	printers	Dublin	1968–71	receipt book

DUB 84	P. Holland	manufacturing agent	Dublin	1935–50	account books
DUB 86	Bishop & Co.	sack manufacturers	Dublin	1928–80	cash books, ledgers, journals, wages books
DUB 87	Hortons	gents outfitters	Dublin	1925–85	accounts, miscellaneous material
DUB 88	Catholic Defence Association and Catholic Defence League	religious association	Dublin	1902–14	minutes and accounts
DUB 89	McBirney & Co. Ltd	department store	Dublin	1830–1983	minute books, account books, correspondence, invoices deeds and leases
DUB 90	W. & C. McDonnell Ltd	food manufacturers	Dublin	1895–1965	share material, company history deeds etc.
DUB 92	Charles J. Holohan	solicitor	Dublin	1910–	repair books, sales books
DUB 94	Ganter Brothers Ltd	watchmakers and jewellers	Dublin	1905–70	minute books, rule books, correspondence, files etc.
DUB 96	Eblana Loan and Investment Society	loan and investment society	Dublin	1870–1971	minute books, register of boys, account books, printed reports, correspondence, photographs
DUB 98	Harding Boys Home, Lord Edward Street	boys' home	Dublin	1876–1987	audited accounts, minute books, cash books, ledgers, journals, wages books, correspondence, sample books etc.
DUB 101	Hill's Mills	woollen manufacturers	Lucan	1890–1987	account books, minute books, wages books, operational records
DUB 115	Johnston, Mooney & O'Brien	bakers and confectioners	Dublin	1868–	private ledger
DUB 116	Irish Headwear Co. Ltd	wholesale warehousemen	Dublin	1947–58	account books, wages books, operational books
DUB 118	Swiftbrook Paper Mills	paper mill	Saggart	1881–	

Catalogue number	Name	Industry sector	Local area	Period	Other notes
DUB 120	James Adams & Sons	auctioneers and valuers	Dublin	20th century	valuations
DUB 121	Robert E. Turbett & Sons	wholesale wine merchants	Dublin	1930–	account books, sales day books, purchases books
DUB 123	Robert Smyth & Sons Ltd	grocers, wine and cigar merchants	Dublin	1822–3	day books, microfilm
DUB 124	Leverett & Frye	grocers and wine merchants	Ranelagh	1912–27	wages book, microfilm
DUB 126	R. Perry & Co. Ltd	ship chandler	Dun Laoghaire	1911–78	account books, quotations books
DUB 128	Odlum Ltd	millers		1881–	minute books; account books also Odlums (Sallins) Ltd, W.P.& R. Odlum Ltd, Dublin Port Milling Co. Ltd, National Flour Mills Ltd, Irish Grain Ltd, Procea Ltd, Johnson, Mooney & O'Brien Ltd, Dublin Silo Co. Ltd, Euroglas Ltd, W.&G.T. Pollexfen & Co. Ltd
DUB 129	Pigott & Co. Ltd	musical instrument makers	Dublin	19th century–	minute books, agenda book, private ledgers, legal documentation
DUB 130	Kylemore Bakery	bakery	Dublin	1930–42	audited accounts
DUB 131	Irish Cinemas Ltd	cinema	Dublin	1912–	
DUB 132	McHugh Himself	bicycle and cycle agents	Dublin	1932–	cycle and radio sales book
DUB 133	Cullen's Medical Hall	pharmacist	Dublin	20th century	prescription books
DUB 138	Irish Newlaids Ltd	egg wholesalers	Dublin	1934–	administrative and operational records
DUB 139	Pim Brothers	drapers and textile manufacturers	Dublin	20th century	account correspondence

DUB 143	Dock Holdings Ltd	dock holdings	Dublin	20th century	administrative records
DUB 143	P.F. Higgins & Son	auctioneers	Cork and Dublin	1919–27	credit ratings book, newspaper cuttings, book regarding flour and grain prices
DUB 144	Bramerton Holdings Ltd	holding company	Dublin	20th century	administrative records
DUB 144	Francis Casey & Co. Ltd	flour mills	Leixlip	20th century	administrative records
DUB 144	City Quay Investment Co. Ltd	investments	Dublin	20th century	administrative records
DUB 144	Collinstor Trustee Co. Ltd	investments	Dublin	20th century	administrative records
DUB 144	Dollardstown Holdings Ltd	holding company	Dublin	20th century	administrative records
DUB 144	Fahagh Estates Ltd	land/estate	Dublin	20th century	administrative records
DUB 144	Fitzpatricks Footwear Ltd	footwear	Dublin	20th century	administrative records
DUB 144	Fuel Importers (Éire) Ltd	fuel importers		20th century	administrative records
DUB 144	Franklin Investment Ltd	investments		20th century	administrative records
DUB 144	The Gaiety Theatre Co. Ltd	theatre		20th century	administrative records
DUB 144	H. & A. Holdings Ltd	holding company		20th century	administrative records
DUB 144	Kerry Steel Ball Co. Ltd	precision ball bearings	Tralee	20th century	administrative records
DUB 144	Kildare Holdings Ltd	holding company	Dublin	20th century	administrative records
DUB 144	H.O. Loechser (Éire) Ltd	printers	Dublin	20th century	administrative records
DUB 144	Morehampton Properties Ltd	property	Dublin	20th century	administrative records
DUB 144	Munster & Leinster Estates Ltd	property	Dublin	20th century	administrative records
DUB 145	F. Barrett & Co.	lighthouse engineers	Dublin	1860–	letter books, account books and operational records
DUB 146	McCullough Pigott Ltd	musical instrument dealers	Dublin	1941–	piano sales book, various administrative records
DUB 147	Milltown Tontine and Benefit Society	charity	Dublin	20th century	administrative records

Catalogue number	Name	Industry sector	Local area	Period	Other notes
DUB 149	S.L. Hutchinson	agent of the Hutchinson Tyre Co. and the County Chemical Co.	Dublin	1908–10	business correspondence
DUB 150	Grimes	shipping, fishing and potato business	Rush	1830s–	account books
DUB 154	Limerick Steamship Co., British and Irish Steam Packet Co., Clyde Shipping Co.	shipping	Limerick	1872–1958	financial papers, accounts and correspondence
DUB 155	Dublin Cross Channel Shipping Association	shipping		1954–	minutes and related papers
DUB 156	Cooney Jennings Ltd	builders	Dublin	20th century	operational and administrative records
DUB 157	Irish Wools Ltd	woolen merchants	Dublin	1919–33	private ledger
DUB 158	Irish Wools Ltd	woolen merchants	Dublin	1832–67	general ledger
DUB 159	Maxwell, Weldon & Co.	solicitors	Dublin	1920	letter book
DUB 160	Royal Insurance Co.	insurance company	Dublin	1913–	operational and administrative records
DUB 161	Irish Gown (Manufacturers) Ltd	clothing manufacturers	Dublin	1931–	minute books, account books, correspondence
DUB 163	Building & Allied Trades Union	trade union	Dublin	20th century	administrative and operational records
DUB 165	Sherry Fitzgerald Ltd	auctioneers and valuers	Dublin	20th century	operational records
DUB 172	Quinn Enamellers	enamellers	Dublin	1934–66	minute books and operational records
DUB 173	St Vincent de Paul Conference of St Francis of Assisi	charity	Dublin	1905–	minute books and operational records
DUB 174	C. Cosgrove & Sons	cattle salesmen	Dublin	1912–21	sales books for Dublin Cattle Market

Reference	Name	Type	Location	Date	Records
DUB 175	Grand Chapter of Order of Black Pirates	social club	Dublin	1917–26	minute book
DUB 177	Alliance & Dublin Gas Consumers Co.	gas consumers company	Dublin	1836–	minute books, account books, operational records, maps, plans and drawings
DUB 181	Marketing Image Ltd	design and advertising consultants	Dublin	20th century	administrative, financial advertising and operational records
DUB 182	Matthew O'Byrne, Fountain Head Foundry	bell founders	Dublin	1840–1974	administrative and operational records, photographs
DUB 182	Sheridan Brothers, Eagle Foundary	bell founders	Dublin	1860–1974	records
DUBLIN 2004/87	Patrick J. Fox	Parnellite	Dublin	20th century	papers and photographs regarding family and political matters
DUBLIN 2004/94	Central Dairies, Upper Stephen Street	grocers	Dublin	c.1950s	grocery account book regarding goods bought by Mrs Mary Dunne
DUBLIN 2004/119	Dillon's Bank	bank	Dublin	1748–52	bills payable and receivable books, 1 box
DUBLIN 2004/126	Michael Gorman	tourist industry		20th century	reports, photographs and publications relating to the Irish tourist industry, 20 boxes
DUBLIN 2004/127	Brewers, Distillers & General Labourers Social Club	social club	Dublin	20th century	minute books and accounts, 5 boxes
DUBLIN 2005/55	Johnston, Mooney & O'Brien	bakers	Dublin	1889–	minute books
DUBLIN 2005/58	An Óige	youth association		1931–	minute books, files, publications, photographs, 41 boxes

Catalogue number	Name	Industry sector	Local area	Period	Other notes
DUBLIN 2005/87	M.V. Killarney	shipping	Dublin	c.1962	plans and drawings
DUBLIN 2005/164	Dublin Union	health institution	Dublin	20th century	ledgers orders and account books, 5 boxes
	Dublin Corporation, Health Services Section and Tuberculosis Section	local government	Dublin		
DUBLIN 2005/167	Irish Kennel Club	kennel club	Dublin	20th century	transfers of ownership books, c.200 boxes
DUBLIN 2006/86	Dublin House of Industry and the House of Industry Hospitals	hospital	Dublin	1772–1943	minute books, 20 boxes
DUBLIN 2006/96	Monkstown Hospital (Rathdown Hospital)	hospital	Monkstown	1848–	administrative and operational records, 8 boxes
	Rathdown Dispensary	dispensary	Rathdown	1812–23	dispensary journal
	Rathdown Fever Hospital	hospital	Rathdown	1835–74	minute book
DUBLIN 2006/97	Mercer's Hospital	hospital	Dublin	1736–	administrative and operational records, 31 boxes
DUBLIN 2006/98	Royal City of Dublin Hospital	hospital	Dublin, Baggot Street	1878–	administrative and operational records, 100 boxes
DUBLIN 2006/99	Jervis Street Hospital/The Charitable Infirmary	hospital	Dublin, Jervis Street	20th century	operational records, 44 boxes
DUBLIN 2006/101	Queen's Institute of District Nursing in Ireland	nursing	Dublin	1889–	administrative and operational records, 24 boxes
DUBLIN 2006/105	William Laird & Co. Ltd, The Nelson Pharmacy	pharmacy	Dublin, 69 Upper Sackville Street	1898–1954	annual accounts, correspondence, receipts, 1 box

DUBLIN 2006/106	Dublin Docklands Authority	port authority	Dublin	20th century	minute books 10 boxes
DUBLIN 2006/107	Pembroke School	school	Dublin, Pembroke Rd	20th century	roll books, files, 8 boxes
EX1/1–2		Memoranda rolls			Export controls including the value of exports. Inventories of personal, household and agricultural goods (usually required for the payment of debts on death)
GAL2/1/1	Sweeney Brothers	solicitors	East Galway		Hibernian Bank and A.D. Comyn, solicitors (Loughrea), Ballinasloe garage
GAL 3	Timothy Naughton & Co.	merchant and builders' suppliers	Galway	early 20th century	account books, bills
GAL 5		carpenter	Galway	1899–1904	
GAL 8	Glynn's Hotel	hotel	Gort	1947–59	account books, visitors' books
GAL 9	Fahy's	chemists	Galway	20th century	prescription books
GALWAY 2006/108	Day's Hotel	hotel	Inishbofin	20th century	accounts, 4 boxes
KER 1	O'Neill	hardware merchant	Killarney	c.1920–c.1940	account book
KER 9	J.M. Reidy	apothecary	Tralee	1855–76	
KER 10	K. McMahon	general merchant	Killarney	1897–1962	account books
KERR 12		tea, wine and spirit merchants	Ballyheigue	1881–1961	account books
KERR 12	Palmer & Co.	creamery	Ballyheigue	1898–1929	account books
KERRY 14	Kerry Fashions Ltd	knitwear	Tralee	20th century	administrative, financial and operational manufacturers records
KERRY 2004/128	Dr Samuel Kerr	apothecary	Tarbert	18th century	draft appeal for assistance after premises were burnt down by Whiteboys, 1 item

Catalogue number	Name	Industry sector	Local area	Period	Other notes
KK 1	Mulhall	grocer and baker	Kilkenny	1889–1959	
KK 3	Crotty	bakers	Kilkenny	1922–58	
KK 4	Nolan	general merchant	Goresbridge	1873–1915	
KK 5	Patrick Grace	grocer and publican	Ballyragget	1912–1973	counter books, day books, ledgers
KK 12	Bowden	grocer, bar, hardware	Urlingford	1869–1939	
KK 18	O'Connor	watch sale and repair	Kilkenny	1886–1939	
KK 21	DeLoughrey	garage, hardware	Kilkenny	1886–1939	
KK 30	Darcy & Sons	cabinet maker, undertaker, grocery and bar	Kilkenny	1869–1919	
KK 33		Tanyard	Thomastown	1845–1916	account book
KK 37	Cushendale Woollen Mills	wool and grain milling	Graignamanagh	1841–1956	farm accounts Clifden, Burtchaell and Farmer estate accounts
KK 38	Langrishe family		Knocktopher	1639–1911	correspondence and estate accounts
KK 39	Hughes	hardware merchant	Graignamanagh	1858–1907	business records
KK 45		hatter		1738–92	account book
KK 46	Kilkenny Design Workshops Ltd			1965–	accounts, reports, correspondence, operational record
KLD 11	McCabe	butcher	Monasterevan	1876–85	accounting records
KLD 18	Kildare Wallpapers Ltd			1936–62	ledger
KLD 21	E.A. Coonan & Sons	auctioneers and valuers	Maynooth	1922–48	
KLD 22	Samuel Holmes Ltd	engineers	Monasterevan	1920s	account books, files, catalogues
KLD 22	Samuel Holmes Ltd	engineers	Monasterevan	20th century	account books
KLD 23	Celbridge Mills Ltd	milling	Celbridge	1940–	minute books, account books, correspondence
LEIT 1	Killegar estate and Godley family			1667–1906	

LEIT 4	Gannon	footwear retailer and drapers	Mohill	1906–24	wages books, accounts, files
LEIT 5	Shannon Industries Ltd	toy manufacturers	Carrick-on-Shannon	20th century	account books, correspondence, diaries
LEIX 28	W.J. Morrissey	publican and vintner	Abbeyleix	1834–	ledger
LFD 4/9		haulage firm		1837–9	
LIM 1	M. Maguire	import business	Garryspillane	1887–1923	farm account books
LIM 2	Tinsley	flour milling	Limerick	1866–1964	mills Limerick and Croom
LIM 3	James H. Roche		Limerick	1901–37; 1843–7	also an apothecary's ledger
LIM 6	John Clune Ltd	tobacco and snuff manufacturers	Limerick	1908–64	
LIM 11	F. Casey	cycle agent	Rathkeale	1905–42	
LIM 21	Ranks (Ireland) Ltd	milling		1840–79	audited accounts, minutes, account books, files, maps, plans and drawings; includes the records and drawings of James Bannatyne & Sons Ltd, J.N. Russell Ltd, J. & R. Webb Ltd, Cork Milling Co. Ltd, Joseph Hosford Ltd, Shannon Silo Co. Ltd, Irish Bakeries Ltd, J.W. McMullen Ltd, Bennett & Co. Ltd, South of Ireland Grain Transport Co. Ltd, John Furlong and Sons (1932) Ltd, T. Hallinan and Sons (1932) Ltd, M.J. & L. Goodbody Ltd, C.M.C. Holdings Ltd, Dublin North Milling Co. Ltd, Thomas Swan and Co., Blue Cross Ltd, Cork and District Flour Millers Association, Ranks (Ireland) Sales Ltd

Catalogue number	Name	Industry sector	Local area	Period	Other notes
LIM 22	Ranks Mills	flour milling	Limerick, Clara	1846–	including Limerick and Clara Mills
LIM 22	Shaw and Co.	meat and bacon factors	Limerick	1925–72	register of members, accounts
LIM 26	Leen's Hotel	hotel	Abbeyfeale	20th century	operational and administrative records
LIM 28	Limerick Shipping Co.	shipping	Limerick	1940–70	minute books, agenda books, company registers
LIM 28	Philip O'Donovan Ltd	mineral water manufacturers	Limerick	1940–9	minute book
LIMERICK 2005/70	Ancient Order of Foresters	men's association	Limerick City, Garryowen Court	1898–1919	minute book, account books, reports and correspondence, 5 boxes
LON 10		dispensary	Edgeworthstown	1835–41	register photocopy
LON 11	Denniston family	farmers	Drummaross	1792–1923	farm account books, family papers
LON 12	James Fagin	cattle dealer	Moatefarrell	1861–77	cattle sales book
LON 14	Longford Gas Co.	gas company	Longford	1922–5	works book, minute books, register of shareholders, account book microfilm
LOU 1	Carroll	grocer, bar, undertaker	Dunleer	1865–1911	Account books
LOU 3, 4, 7	Several Dundalk firms from three local solicitors' practices	solicitors	Dundalk	1896–1923	
LOU 8	*Dundalk Democrat*	printers	Louth	1890–1958	including account books of 2 local firms, 1807–22, 1857–58
LOU 13	Ancient Order of Hibernians (Board of Erin)	men's association		1906–82	minute books, printed journals, correspondence, accounts
LOU 14	Clarkes (Ireland) Ltd	shoemakers	Louth	1936–82	accounts, reports, correspondence
LOU 15	Thomas Williamson Ltd	timber importers and builders providers	Louth	1850–1984	bank book, private ledgers, accounts, invoices, correspondence
LOU 16	Irish National Foresters	foresters	Dundalk	1895–1945	legal papers, correspondence, rule book
LOU 17	United Irish League	political association	Dundalk	1903–05	minute book

Ref	Name	Business	Location	Dates	Records
LOU 18	Ancient Order of Hibernians (Drogheda)	men's association	Drogheda	1918–82	accounts, correspondence, minutes
LOU 20	Rogers	pub and grocery	Barmeath	1860s–	day books, family papers
LOU 21	Bellew and Bryan families	landed estates	Barmeath Castle and Jenkinstown	1720–1865	account books (microfilm)
LOU 22	Ardee Dispensary	dispensary	Ardee	1814–39	account book microfilm
LOU 23	John Halliday & Son Ltd	footwear manufacturers	Dundalk	1928–70	agreement and printed accounts
LOU 24	J. Berrill	grocer and egg merchant	Drogheda	1897–	cash books, stock books, letter books, egg account books
LOU 25	P.J. Carroll & Co. Ltd	tobacco	Dundalk	1938–	administrative and operational records
LX 5	Gibney	maltings	Portlaoise	1867–1972	
MAYO 3	Foxford Woollen Mills	woollen mills		1896–1939	
MAYO 5		grocery	Westport	1883–1923	day books
MAYO 6		undertaker	Westport	1841–55, 1905–10	ledgers
MAYO 7	Wynne	newsagent and photographer	Castlebar	1879–1947	account books
MAYO 10	Higgins	bar and grocery	Kilkelly	1879–1921	day books
MAYO 12		harbour commissioners	Westport	1855–1952	
MAYO 13	Lucan Estate		Westport	1835–73	rent ledgers
MAYO 14	John McGing	grocery and bar	Westport	1874–1935	sales and purchases books
MAYO 15	John Gibbons	emigration agent	Westport	1907–42	emigration books
MAYO 16	Mrs Burns, Temperance Hotel	hotel	Westport	1927–33	account books
MAYO 17	Breege Walsh	publican	Westport	1893–1954	ledger and spirit stock book, spirit stock book, 1893–1966
MAYO 18	P.J. Henehan	publican	Westport	1938–51	cash receipts book, ledger, 1946–8

Catalogue number	Name	Industry sector	Local area	Period	Other notes
MAYO 19	Tom Navin	general contractor and undertaker	Westport	1901–50	wages books, day books, letters
MAYO 19	Tom Navin	building contractor and undertaker	Westport	1904–	account books
MAYO 20	Rileys & Boland	timber merchants/ builders providers	Ballina	1928–70	sales books, estimates books
MAYO 22	Castlebar Bacon Co. Ltd	food manufacturers	Castlebar	1935–	account books, operational books
MAYO 23	P. Higgins & Son	publican and grocer	Kilkelly	1900	day book
MAYO 24	M. Mulloy & Sons	grocers, ironmongers and importers	Westport	1859–	account books, letter books
MAYO 25	Messrs Carey Walsh Ltd	grocers, drapers, sawmillers and hardware merchants	Newport	1909–49	account books and correspondence
MEATH 6	Keoghan family	farm	Navan	1855–84	farm account book
MEATH 8	Ward family	farm	Slane	1876–78	farm account book of Steward
MEATH 9	McDonnell	bakers	Clonee	1796–1910	account books and papers
MON 5	Monaghan County Infirmary	infirmary	Ballybay	1886–90	bread delivery book, 1903–4; day book
MONAGHAN 2006/100			Monaghan	1768–1857	minute book/ account book, 1 box
OFF 5	Egan Tarleton	malsters	Tullamore	1910–69	
OFF 7	Scully	grocer, grain merchant	Kilcormac	1890–1964	
OFF 9	Clara & Belmont Mills (Perry family)	mills	Kilcormac	1843–1967	
OFF 12	J. & L.F. Goodbody Ltd	jute, sack and twine manufacturers	Clara	1846–1962	minute books, diaries, account books
OFF 12	J. & L.F. Goodbody	jute, sack and twine manufacturers	Clara	1891–	deeds, leases, insurance policies

Ref	Company/Name	Type	Location	Date	Description
OFF 13	G.N. Walsh Ltd	motor engineers	Offaly	1917–22	work sheets and work books, receipts and invoices
OFF 15	Irish National Forresters Ltd	forestry	Offaly	1938–70 20th century	minute books, operational records, photographs Conn of the Hundred Battles' Branch
OFF 16	Goodbody & Kennedy	solicitors	Offaly	1862–	accounts, correspondence
OFF 17	Arthur Guinness	agency	Birr	1900–	operational and financial records
RC8/1–43		Royal Commission calendar			price controls organization of royal demesne manors and financial relations between them and the exchequer
ROS 11	McDonnell	landed estates	Mount Talbot	1898–1972	farm accounts
ROS 13	Hodson Estate	mills		1787–1832	farm account book
SL 11	Collooney Mills		Collooney	1858–69	account book of Stonehall meal shop
SL 14	Jones family	property, rentals, accounts	Ardnaree	1660–1940	
SLIGO 16	Martin Timmoney	grocer	Cliffoney	1902–72	day books, customers ledgers, invoices
TIPP 1	Bourke	draper	Carrick-on-Suir	1807–1958	
TIPP 2	Hollyford Co-op	co-op	Hollyford	1903–71	
TIPP 11	Glenbaun	farm	Clonmel	1878–9	farm account book
TIPP 12		land surveyor		1878–9	account book and diary
TIPP 13	Devlin Medical Hall	pharmacy	Thurles	1898–1963	audited accounts, correspondence, day books, income and expenditure books 1915–62
TIPP 14	Hamill	grocer and publican	Cloughjordan	1916–73	accounts
TIPP 16	Walsh	auctioneers	Templemore	1909–29	auction books
TIPP 26	Shee & Hawe	auctioneers	Carrick-on-Suir	1920–46	
TIPP 27	Roscrea Loan Fund Society	Loan Fund Society	Roscrea	1897–1961	

Catalogue number	Name	Industry sector	Local area	Period	Other notes
TIPP 32	Clonmel Foods Ltd	food manufacturers		1928–78	minute books, accounts, correspondence
TIPP 33	Roscrea Meat Products	food manufacturers		1935–	minutes and accounts
TIPP 37	Ballypatrick Co-operative & Dairy Society	co-operative	Ballypatrick	1913–70	administrative and operational records
WAT 5	Waterford Gas Company	gas company	Waterford	1892–1964	
WAT 8	Malcolmson's	mill	Portlaw	1795–8, 1830–5	
WAT 24	Doolan	publican and whiskey blender		1898–1944	
WAT 26	Clover Meats Ltd	food manufacturers		1927–78	account books, operations books, correspondence files
WAT 27	Irish Tanners Ltd	leather tanning	Portlaw	1920–80	cash books, ledgers, operational books, correspondence, inventories and valuations; also includes records of Gorey Leather Co., New Ross Tanning Co., Dungarvan Leather Ltd, Dickens Leather Co., Ollafur Ltd, Irish Wools Ltd, Donegal Hide and Skin Co., Plunder & Pollack Ltd, Goliath Belting Co., Waterford Leathers Ltd
WAT 28	Waterford Harbours Commissioners	harbour commissioners	Waterford	1918–60	pilot stations returns books, vouchers books, duties books, letter books, account books
WAT 28		harbour commissioners	Waterford	1816–	minute books, letter books, account books, dues books, arrival and departures books, engineers' files, legal documentation maps, plans and drawings
WAT 30	Clyde Shipping Co.	shipping		1889–1975	wages books, operational books and files

Ref	Name	Type	Location	Dates	Records
WAT 31	Graves & Co. Ltd	builders providers	Waterford	1813–1973	audited accounts, account books, operational documentation, plans drawings, correspondence including and Waterford Brick Co., Ballingarry Cola Mining Co., William Graves & Son, J.P. Graves & Co., Patent Roofing Co.
WAT 33	R. & H. Hall	grain merchants	Waterford	1897–1974	account books
WAT 34	Patrick. J. Walsh	public works contractor	Tramore	1942–85	costings regarding water, drainage and sewerage schemes
WEX 2			Ballycashlane, near Broadway	1800–67	accounts, including farm accounts
WEX 3		bar and undertaker	Wellington-bridge	1887–88	
WEX 4	Phelan		Carrick-on-Bannow	1878–90	farm account book
WEX 7	Carleys Bridge Pottery	pottery	Enniscorthy	1905–76	correspondence, personal papers, notes photocopies
WEX 9	Cloney's	mills	Ballinboola	1792–1939	
WEX 11	P.J. Roche & Sons	malsters	New Ross	1859–1966	
WEX 15	Rossiter family	general merchant, bar and post office	Kilmuckridge	1775–1825	farm account book
WEX 16				1831–1909	
WEX 20	Elmes family		Robinstown	1770–	farm account, bills, receipts, family papers
WEX 21	Messrs. Galvin Bros	nursery	Wexford	1940–67	sales books
WEX 22	Pat Delaney	farmer	Brocarra, Adamstown	1889–1956	bills and receipts

Catalogue number	Name	Industry sector	Local area	Period	Other notes
WEX 23	Clover Meats Ltd	food manufacturers	Wexford	1916–79	minute books, account books, operations books, photographs; includes records of the Wexford Meat Supply and Bacon Factory Ltd
WEX 25	P.L. & J. Meehan	motor agent	Erinvale	1912–52	bills and receipts
WEXFORD 2006/102	P. Byrne	Grocer, baker, flour merchant	Enniscorthy	1893–	account books, correspondence, 8 boxes
WICK 3	Fogarty family & Aughrim Mill	Mills		1738–1903	
WICK 8	Brennan	dressmaker	Carnew	1930–53	account book
WICK 26	Irish National Foresters		Bray	1903–82	minutes, accounts, loose correspondence
WICK 27	Mrs McGuire	chemist		1949–	prescription books, accounts
WICK 29		grocery	Wicklow	1861–63	account book
WICK 30	Morrin & Son Ltd	millers	Baltinglass	1850–1982	account books, memorandum books, correspondence
WICK 31	Frank Donnelly	draper	Bray	1950–65	account books
WICK 32	Joseph Healy		Roundwood	1927–33	sports club account book
WICK 32	Joseph Healy		Roundwood	1952–61	ploughing match account book
WICK 33	Stephen G. Gallagher	county surveyor	Wicklow	1931	notes on roads in the Irish Free State
WM 1	Wilson's Hospital	school	Bunbrosna	1768–1966	
WM 9	Ogle family		Delvin	1846–1932	house and farm records
WM 18	Athlone	loan fund		1846–8	ledger

Reference	Name	Type	Town/County	Date	Records/Other notes
AG 61	Agricultural Wages Board			1940–83	minutes (9 volumes)
CR/1/92	Killead Church of Ireland	registers	Co. Antrim	1828–1997	
CR/1/93	Gartree Church of Ireland	registers	Co. Antrim	1938–67	
CR/1/94	RAF chaplaincy, Aldergrove	registers	Co. Antrim	1940–56	
CR/5/19	Bailies Mills Reformed Presbyterian Church	church	Down	1844–1974	financial records; also includes other church records
CR/5/5	Reformed Presbyterian Church in Ireland	records		1876–1985	Including records of the Reformed Presbyterian Mission to Antioch, Syria, 1886–1970
CR/6/13	Donegall Square Methodist Church	church	Belfast	1915–95	accounts
D. 1050/13	Ulster Farmers' Union	farmers' union		1918–88	minute books etc.
D. 1050/20	Amalgamated Society of Woodworkers	workers' union	Newtownards	1890–1967	account books, minute books
D. 1050/6	Belfast and District Trades Union Council	trade union		1925–34	minute books etc.
D. 1928 add.	William Brownlow	estate	Lurgan	1752–4	estate and household account
D. 2784/23	Downshire estates	estate	Antrim and Down	1744–1930	rent rolls and cash books
D. 2784/23	Deramore estates	estate	Down	1939–69	cash book
D. 2805 add.	Harland & Wolff	shipbuilders	Belfast	1961–89	board reports, insurance papers etc.
D. 2966/104	Harland & Wolff	shipbuilders	Belfast	1872	apprenticeship indenture
D. 3059 add	Moneymore Co-operative & Agricultural Society	co-op		1911–71	account books, statement of account

Reference	Name	Type	Town/County	Date	Records/Other notes
D. 3622 add.	Samuel and John Cunningham	grain millers	Shankill Road	1844–66	correspondence and accounts
D. 3741 add.	John Gunning & Son Ltd	linen manufacturers and finishers	Cookstown, Co. Tyrone	1939–55	balance sheets and correspondence
D. 3741 add.	Wellbrook Mill	mill	Tyrone	1934–54	wages books
D. 3849 add.	Royal Ulster Agricultural Society, North-Eastern Agricultural Society of Ireland and the Large White Ulster Pig Society	co-ops	Belfast (Down, Antrim, Armagh Monaghan)	1897–1937	minute books and correspondence
D. 3872	Ritchie Hart & Co. Ltd	manufacturers of heavy machinery	Belfast	1878–1984	inventory and valuation, register of shareholders, correspondence, minutes of directors' meetings
D. 3893	Wolfhill Spinning Co.	spinning	Belfast	1869–1958	business records
D. 3893	Ulster Spinning Co.	spinning	Belfast	1869–1958	business records
D. 3893	Grove Spinning Co.	spinning	Belfast	1869–1958	business records
D. 3895	Belfast Co-operative Society Ltd	co-op	Belfast	1889–1983	business records
D. 3895	Lisburn Co-operative Society Ltd	co-op	Lisburn	1889–1983	business records
D. 3895	Irish Co-operative Society Ltd	co-op		1889–1963	business records
D. 3900	James Buckley & Sons	builders	Belfast	1931–53	purchases ledgers, sales ledgers, cash books
D. 3901	Donegall Place Association	association of Belfast traders	Belfast	1961–8	minutes
D. 3912	Antrim Light and Power Co.	electricity generators	Antrim	1934–50	minute book

					business records
D. 3920	East Downshire Steam Ship Co. Ltd	steamship owners, sawmillers, importers of coal, timber, slates, fireclay goods and cement	Ballynahinch	1847–1980	
D. 3964	James A. Mackie & Sons	machine manufacturers	Belfast	1892–1983	cash books, ledgers, journals, wage books etc.
D. 3981	Eason & Son Ltd	wholesale and retail newsagent	Belfast	1825–1977	minute book, ledgers, journals, cash books, wages books
D. 3990	J.&T.M. Greeves	estate	Londonderry	1775–93	account book
D. 3997		flax spinners	Belfast	1951–60	records
D. 4063	Belfast Association of Engineers	professional association	Belfast	1962–91	records
D. 4064	Gill's Charity	charity	Carrickfergus, Co. Antrim	1768–1927	account and minute book; note: charity formed by thewill of Henry Gill(1761) to support 'fourteen aged men decayed in their circumstances'
D.1857 add.	Belfast Chamber of Commerce	Chamber of Commerce	Belfast	1918–58 & 1963–82	annual reports and printed journals
D. 3531 add.	Shirley estate	estate	Carrickmacross, Co. Monaghan	1814–1919	accounts, leases, workers' time books
D/1051/21	Union of Construction, Allied Trades and Technicians	trade union		1878–1983	minute books, account books; note: comprising the Amalgamated Society of Carpenters and Joiners, Amalgamated Union of Cabinetmakers
D/1503	Earl Annesley	estate	Castlewellan, Co. Down	1813–1918	estate rentals and cashbooks

Reference	Name	Type	Town/County	Date	Records/Other notes
D/2638	Needham	estate	Newry and Mourne	1821–1920	rentals; Kilmorey estate
D/3590	Agnes Skrine née Higginson [Moira O'Neill]	literary manuscripts		1879–1924	
D/3814	Northern Ireland Branch of the Library Association	records		1929–90	
D/3994/5	Ulster Banking Co.	bank	Belfast	1836–8	correspondence with Messrs. Perkins, Bacon and French (solicitors)
D/4155	Professor Black	economic and social historian	Belfast	c.1975–85	papers
D/4166	Blackers' Mill	linen manufacturers	Portadown	1920–97	business records
D/4189	Andrews' Flax Mill	flax milling	Comber, Co. Down	1863–1970	letter books, ledgers, report books, stock books, pay books and wage books
D/4228	Belfast City Museum and Art Gallery	museum	Belfast	1888–1965	correspondence, financial records, publications, architectural plans
D/4233	Armar Corry	estate	Antrim, Down and Fermanagh	1886–1928	rentals
D/4256	Braid Water Spinning Mill	milling	Ballymena	1860–1970	records
D/4256	Moygashel Mills	milling	Tyrone	1860–1970	minute books, order books, accounts and annual reports
D/4261	Albion Clothing Co.	clothing company	Belfast	1890–1970	business and financial papers

Reference	Name	Type	Location	Date	Description
D/4266	Denis Rebbeck	Harland & Wolff Chairman		1950–80	business and personal papers financial records; also includes a range of trademarks
D/4272	Barbours Threads	mill	Hilden, Co. Antrim		
D/4275	Pharmaceutical Society of Northern Ireland	professional society		1925–92	minute books and correspondence
D/4277	Richard Robinson	archbishop	Armagh	1763	patent from George III
D/4280	McCready & Ewart families		Belfast	c.1890–1970	family papers
D/4282	Northern Ireland Athletics Federation	athletics federation	Belfast	1934–96	minute books and annual reports
D/4286	North Cricket Club	cricket club	Belfast	1862–2000	scorebooks, annual reports, accounts, fixture lists, visitor books, scrapbooks
D/4294	Robert Hogg & Co. Ltd		Donegall Square, Belfast	1907–75	financial papers; also includes John Magee & Co. Ltd
D/4363	Falls Flax Spinning Co.		Belfast	1865–1934	
D/4367	Killyleagh True Blues Loyal Orange Lodge No. 59	records	Co. Down	1856–1985	
	Kildoag Loyal Orange Lodge No. 1164		Co. Londonderry	1929–2002	
D/4370	Know family, Earls of Ranfurly	working papers		c.1780–1920	
D/4372	Jeffrey Dudgeon		Belfast	1922–2005	papers relating to the book *Roger Casement: the Black Diaries – with a study of his background, sexuality and Irish political life*
D/4376	Murray, Son & Co.	tobacco manufacturers	Belfast	1884–1970	

Reference	Name	Type	Town/County	Date	Records/Other notes
D/4377	Thomas Percy, Bishop of Dromore (1729–1811)	personal papers		1774–c.1812	
D/4380	Maguire & Herbert Richard Herbert	solicitors wine and spirit merchants	Enniskillen	1877–1980	
D/4381	McCaw, Allen & Co.	linen manufacturers	Lurgan	c.1880–1992	
D/4382	Rev. George Good	personal papers	Sri Lanka and Northern Ireland	1928–87	
D/4400	Derek Hill	personal papers	Churchill, Co. Donegal	1934–2000	
LGBD 2	Local Government Board		Dublin	c.1890–c.1907	precedent book; workhouse administration and poor relief
MIC/1/341	Down Cathedral	cathedral	Co. Down	1730–1870	one chapter book, three rentals, one Cathedral Committee improvements account book, one lease and a translation of the Charter
MIC/683	W.H. Welpy	wills	Greenisland, Co. Antrim	early 17th–mid-19th century	c.1500 abstracts of wills
NDR/35/1996	Enterprise Ulster	industrial development		1981–2, 1986–7	annual reports and statements of accounts
NDR/47/1996	Belfast City Gas Department	gas distributors	Belfast	1923–90	records
PTE/10/1997	Belfast Masonic Charities	charity	Belfast	1861–1989	minutes books, cash books, annual reports

PTE /33/1996	Irish Association for Cultural, Economic and Social Relations			1968–95	minutes, accounts, correspondence and press cuttings
RGO 9/1	Northern Ireland Census	census		1991	10 printed reports including economic activity report, housing and house-hold composition, and workplace transport to work, migration, eduction, religion and Irish language
T. 3763; MIC 537	Langford estates	estate	Antrim and Londonderry	1610–1804	accounts, leases, title deeds, rentals
T. 3765	Rawdon estates	estate	Ballynahinch and Moira	c.1630–1781	accounts, rentals, title deeds, tenants' petitions
T. 3818		salt mining	Carrickfergus, Co. Antrim	1894–1994	papers
T/3877	John Tulloch	74th Highland Regiment		1852–9	12 letters relating to the Indian Mutiny

Select bibliography

Anderson, P.A. and J. Rose, *Dictionary of literary biography: volume 106, British literary publishing houses, 1820–1880* (London, 1990)

Annisette, M. and P. O'Regan, 'The survival of an All Ireland institution: the case of the Institute of Chartered Accountants of Ireland', paper presented at the *Critical perspectives in accounting conference*, Apr. 2002, New York, available at http://aux.zicklin.baruch.cuny.edu/critical/

Auditing Practices Board, *International Standard on Auditing (UK & Ireland) 500 Audit Evidence* (London, 2004)

Barnard, Toby, *A guide to sources for the history of material culture in Ireland, 1500–2000* (Dublin, 2005)

Burchell, S., C. Clubb and A.G. Hopwood, 'Accounting in its social context: towards a history of value added in the United Kingdom' in *Accounting, Organizations and Society*, 10 (1985), pp 381–413

Court, W.H.B., 'What is economic history' in W.H.B. Court (ed.), *Scarcity and choice in history* (London, 1970), pp 1–5

Clark, M., *The archives of the Dublin staple, 1596–1678* (Dublin, 1996)

— and R. Refaussé (eds), *Directory of historic Dublin guilds* (Dublin, 1993)

Clarke, P., 'A glimpse at Irish accounting history' in *The Irish Accounting Review*, 3 (2) (1996), pp 23–40

—, 'Financial reporting in Ireland: the period of independent isolation' in *The Irish Accounting Review*, 8 (2) (2001), pp 23–44

Clarkson, L.A., 'Hospitality, housekeeping and high living in eighteenth-century Ireland' in J.R. Hill and C. Lennon (eds), *Luxury and austerity, Historical Studies XXI* (Dublin, 1990), pp 84–105

—, 'Irish social history, 1974–2000 and beyond' in *Irish Economic & Social History*, 28 (2002), pp 1–12

Clyde, T., *Irish literary magazines: an outline history and descriptive biography* (Dublin, 2003)

Crean, T., 'The reorganization of the records of the Irish Bank Officials' Association' in *Saothar*, 27 (2002), pp 112–3

Cullen, L.M., 'Hon. Secretary's report' in *Irish Economic & Social History*, 1 (1974), pp 71–4

—, 'Irish Manuscripts Commission survey of business records' *Irish Economic & Social History*, 10 (1983), pp 81–5

—, *Eason & Son: a history* (Dublin, 1989)

—, *The brandy trade under the ancien régime* (Cambridge, 1998)

—, 'Catholic social classes under the Penal Laws' in T.P. Power and K. Whelan (eds), *Endurance and emergence: Catholics in Ireland in the eighteenth century* (Dublin, 1990), pp 57–84

—, 'Eighteenth-century flour milling in Ireland' in *Irish Economic & Social History*, 4 (1997), pp 5–25

Daly, M.E., *The buffer State: the historical roots of the Department of the Environment* (Dublin, 1997)

—, *The first Department: a history of the Department of Agriculture* (Dublin, 2002)

Dennison, S.R. and O. McDonagh, *Guinness 1886–1939: from incorporation to the Second World War* (Cork, 1998)

Donnelly, B. and M. Ó hÓgartaigh, 'Medical archives for the socio-economic historian' in *Irish Economic & Social History*, 27 (2001), pp 66–72

Dooley T.A.M., *Sources for the history of landed estates* (Dublin, 2000)

—, *The big houses and landed estates of Ireland: a research guide* (Dublin, 2007)

Elton, G.R., *Return to essentials. Some reflections on the current state of historical study* (Cambridge, 1991)

Evans, R.J., *In defence of history* (London, 1997)

Farmar, T., *The legendary lofty clattery café: Bewley's of Ireland* (Dublin, 1988)

—, *A history of Craig Gardner: the first 100 years* (Dublin, 1988)

—, *Holles Street 1894–1994: The National Maternity Hospital – a centenary history* (Dublin, 1994)

—, *Heitons – a managed transition* (Dublin, 1996)

Ferriter, D., *Cuimhnigh ar Luimneach: a history of Limerick County Council, 1898–1998* (Limerick, 1998)

Gilligan, J., 'Murray's of Dunshaughlin, 1896–1910' in D.A. Cronin, J. Gilligan and K. Holton (eds), *Irish fairs and markets – studies in local history* (Dublin, 2001), pp 224–48

Hines, R.D., 'Financial accounting: in communicating reality, we construct reality' in *Accounting, Organizations and Society*, 13:3 (1988), pp 251–61

— and S.R. Moriarity, 'Understanding accounting in its social and historical context' in *Accounting Review*, 65:1 (1990), pp 286–7

Hobsbawm, E., *On history* (London, 1997)

Hogan, D., *The legal profession in Ireland, 1789–1922* (Dublin, 1986)

—, *Brehons, serjeants and attorneys: studies in the history of the Irish legal profession* (Dublin, 1990)

Hogan, R., *Dictionary of Irish literature* (London, 1996)

Hopwood, A.G., 'The archaeology of accounting systems' in *Accounting, Organizations and Society*, 12 (1987), pp 207–34

Hoskin, K. and R. Macve, 'The genesis of accountability: the West Point connections' in *Accounting, Organizations and Society*, 13 (1988), pp 37–73

Jeacle, I. and E. Walsh, 'From moral evaluation to rationalization: accounting and the shifting technologies of credit' in *Accounting Organizations and Society*, 27 (2002), pp 737–61

Lambe, M., 'At the Cross: a shop in rural Ireland, 1880–1911' in D.A. Cronin, J. Gilligan and K. Holton (eds), *Irish fairs and markets: studies in local history* (Dublin, 2001), pp 206–23

Lee, T.A., 'The changing form of the Corporate Annual Report' in *Accounting Historians Journal*, 21:1 (1994), pp 215–34

Loft, A., 'Towards a critical understanding of accounting: the case of cost accounting in the U.K., 1914–1925' in *Accounting, Organizations and Society*, 11 (1986), pp 137–71

Luddy, M., *Women and philanthropy in nineteenth-century Ireland* (Cambridge, 1995)

Magee, S., 'D.A. Chart, 1878–1960: archivist, historian, social scientist' in *History Ireland* (spring 2003), pp 15–18

Marriner, S., 'Company financial statements as source material for business historians' in *Business History*, 22 (1980), pp 203–35

McDowell, R.B., *Land & learning: two Irish clubs* (Dublin, 1993)

Meagher, J., 'Elias Voster: the father of Irish accountancy' in *Journal of the Cork Historical and Archaeological Society*, 99 (1994), pp 111–19

Miller, P., T. Hopper and R. Laughlin, 'The new accounting history: an introduction' in *Accounting, Organizations and Society*, 16:3 (1991), pp 395–403

— and C. Napier, 'Genealogies of calculation' in *Accounting, Organizations and Society*, 18 (1993), pp 631–47

— and T. O'Leary, 'Accounting and the construction of the governable person' in *Accounting, Organizations and Society*, 12 (1987), pp 235–66

Mills, P.A., 'Agency, auditing and the unregulated environment: some further historical evidence' in *Accounting, Auditing and Accountability Journal*, 3:1 (1990), pp 54–66.

Ó Gráda, C., *Black '47 and beyond: the Great Irish Famine in history, economy and memory* (Princeton, NJ, 1999)

Ó hÓgartaigh, C. and M. Ó hÓgartaigh, 'A man's trousers on' in *Accountancy Ireland* (Sept. 1999), pp 22–3

—, 'Teaching accounting in eighteenth-century Ireland' in F. Larkin (ed.), *Librarians, poets and scholars: a festschrift for Dónall Ó Luanaigh* (Dublin, 2007), pp 185–94

Ó hÓgartaigh, M., 'Dr Dorothy Price and the elimination of childhood tuberculosis' in J. Augusteijn (ed.), *Ireland in the 1930s: new perspectives* (Dublin, 1999), pp 67–82

—, *Kathleen Lynn and maternal medicine* (Dublin, 2000)

Ó hÓgartaigh, C., M. Ó hÓgartaigh and I. Jeacle, '"How it essentially was": truth claims in history and accounting' in *Accounting Historians Journal*, 29:1 (2001), pp 42–67

Ohlmeyer, J., 'The statute staple in early modern Ireland: compiling a historical database' in *History Ireland*, 6:4 (winter 1998), pp 36–40

—, 'Calculating debt: the Irish statute staple records' in *Irish Economic & Social History*, 27 (2000), pp 63–5

— and É. Ó Ciardha (eds), *The Irish statute staple books, 1596–1687* (Dublin, 1998)

O'Farrell, P., *The Irish in Australia* (2nd ed., Sydney, 2000)

Oldroyd, D., 'Historiography, causality, and positioning: an unsystematic view of accounting history' in *Accounting Historians Journal*, 26:1 (1999), pp 83–102

Ó Maitiú, S., *W. & R. Jacob: celebrating 150 years of Irish biscuit making* (Dublin, 2001)

O'Sullivan, E. and M. Raftery, *Suffer the little children: the inside story of Ireland's industrial schools* (Dublin, 1999)

Powell, J.S., '*Shot a buck ...*', the Emo estate, 1798–1852. Documents of Portarlington, no. 3 (Portarlington, n.d.)

Reece, B., 'Irish convicts and Australian historians' in B. Reece (ed.), *Irish convicts: the origins of convicts transported to Australia* (Dublin, 1989), pp 1–24

Robinson, H., *A history of accountants in Ireland* (Dublin, 1964)

—, *A history of accountants in Ireland* (Dublin, 1983)

Rose, J. and P.J. Anderson, *Dictionary of literary biography: volume 106, British literary publishing houses, 1881–1965* (London, 1991)

Rowe, D. (ed.), *The Irish chartered accountant: centenary essays, 1888–1988* (Dublin, 1988)

Takei, A., 'The first Irish linen mills, 1800–1824' in *Irish Economic & Social History*, 21 (1994), pp 28–38

Thomas, W.A., *The stock exchanges of Ireland* (Dublin, 1986)

Tosh, J., *The pursuit of history: aims, methods & new directions in the study of modern history* (2nd ed., London, 1991)

Walsh, B., *Roman Catholic nuns in England and Wales, 1800–1937* (Dublin, 2002)

Wall, B.M., *Unlikely entrepreneurs. Catholic sisters and the hospital marketplace, 1865–1925* (Columbus, OH, 2005)

Whitaker, T.K., 'Origins and consolidation, 1783–1826' in F.S.L. Lyons (ed.), *Bicentenary essays, Bank of Ireland* (Dublin, 1983), pp 11–30

Index

Material in appendices 1 and 2 is not featured in the following index.